"It is not in its past that the glories or benefits of the Red Cross lie, but in the possibilities it has created for the future, in the lessons it has taught, in the avenues to humane effort it has opened . . . that shall constitute a bulwark against the mighty woes sure to come sooner or later to all people and all nations."

CLARA BARTON
1904

The
GREATEST MOTHER
in the WORLD

Nurses
the Call from
No Man's Land
is

Nurses of America
humanity
calls you

what is
your answer?

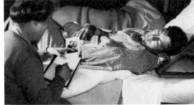

The Red Cross is spending Ten Million
Dollars a Year to help the disabled
ex-service man and his family
ANNUAL ROLL CALL ~ NOV. 11ᵗʰ–24ᵗʰ

GIVE YOUR BLOOD
TO SAVE A LIFE

The
AMERICAN NATIONAL RED CROSS
BLOOD DONOR SERVICE

The
AMERICAN RED CROSS

The First Century

written and edited by
PATRICK F. GILBO

HARPER & ROW, PUBLISHERS, *New York*
Cambridge, Hagerstown, Philadelphia, San Francisco,
London, Mexico City, São Paulo, Sydney

1817

Grateful acknowledgment is made for permission to reprint lines from "Rhymes of a Red Cross Man" from *The Collected Poems of Robert W. Service.* by Robert W. Service. Copyright 1916 by Dodd, Mead and Company, Inc. Copyright renewed 1944 by Robert W. Service. Reprinted by permission of Dodd, Mead and Company, Inc. and McGraw-Hill Ryerson Limited.

Photographs are the property of the American Red Cross unless otherwise noted.

FIRST EDITION

Designer: Ruth Bornschlegel

Library of Congress Cataloging in Publication Data

Gilbo, Patrick F
  The American Red Cross.
  1. Red Cross. United States. American National
Red Cross—History. I. Title.
HV577.G54   361.7′63   80-8204
  ISBN 0-06-011461-4

81 82 83 84 85 10 9 8 7 6 5 4 3 2 1

Contents

Foreword, by Dr. Jerome Holland, Chairman,
American Red Cross   vii

Introduction   ix

1. Growing Pains   1

2. The Age of Innocence   32

3. Expansion and Decline   55

4. Evolution   95

5. Rebirth   142

6. Going Forward   173

7. Threshold to a Second Century   214

Prologue to a New Century, by George M. Elsey, President,
American Red Cross   242

Index   244

A section of color plates follows page 86

Foreword

The largest and most diverse voluntary service organization this nation has ever seen, the American Red Cross has touched the life of virtually every citizen through its array of humanitarian services.

The Red Cross has the advantages of a community-based organization meeting differing, often unique, community needs while at the same time having the strength only a national organization can possess.

I am but one of millions who in the past or the present have volunteered under the Red Cross banner. My involvement provides the satisfaction of knowing that what I do provides benefits to my fellow Americans and to human beings throughout the world.

I am proud to be part of a movement which, through its hundred years, has changed to meet the challenges of emerging social needs, while at the same time maintaining its established services.

Over the past century, millions of Red Cross volunteers have provided a secure foundation of personal and dedicated involvement in a spectrum of programs to aid others in trouble. This strong base, combined with a hundred years of dynamic leadership in humanitarian service, has well prepared the American Red Cross to enter its second century ready to develop and mold its many services to the challenges confronting us as we continue to provide services to people in need—locally, nationally and internationally.

Dr. Jerome Holland, Chairman
American Red Cross

Introduction

A new century challenges the American Red Cross. After one hundred years of service, America's reliance on the Good Neighbor has grown, not lessened. America's needs will continue to be many, but to be effective in the future, the organization must remain strong in the face of changing conditions, and reach out for new horizons in the ways it serves the nation.

Science has failed to harness the fury of the natural elements, and there is still no substitute for the fresh whole blood that sustains life. Men and women in uniform still require emergency leave and personal services to cope with age-old problems; kids still splash through summer swimming lessons to prevent drownings; the elderly and infirm still seek solace and assistance in their battle with loneliness; and the young still look for meaningful ways to share in a dynamic society. Times change, but basic human needs and emotions do not.

The Red Cross offers the willing a chance to lift up someone in genuine need, often someone who has lost all hope. Thousands, hundreds of thousands and—over the many years—millions of people have responded to the challenge: Be of service. Their names range from the not so famous to the likes of John Dos Passos, Ernest Hemingway, Eleanor Roosevelt. Voluntarism is alive, and moneys continue to flow into a myriad of charities despite the toll that inflation levies on the economy. Although the needs and problems of the nation sometimes seem insurmountable, what is life without challenge?

The Red Cross ideal has survived in a land where many other values have seriously eroded. The men and women who follow it have found something invaluable—call it mystique, call it the pioneering spirit, call it love or peace or caring, but don't forget the word "challenge." This book is about the people who have met the challenge, who are meeting it, and who will confront it in the next century of Red Cross service. People made the Red Cross what it is today, and people will move it forward with the nation in the years to come.

As the world grows more complex, it may be that in its next century, the Red Cross will be faced with such tasks as launching rescue operations for galactic colonies in danger of being swallowed up by black holes in space. But whatever the task, one thing, surely, will never change—the reliance of Americans on one another when the chips are down. And that is what the Red Cross is all about. People helping people.

1. Growing Pains

Every history has a starting point. In the case of the American Red Cross, it begins with Clarissa Harlowe Barton, known to the world as Clara Barton, founder of the organization. But no vital organization remains the sole product of one person. The Red Cross of today evolved out of the work and ideas of many people who had the vision to expand upon the New Englander's legacy to humanity.

Barton dominates the early history. She didn't originate the Red Cross idea, nor was she the first person to attempt establishing a Red Cross society in America. She is important because she organized in 1881 a durable society whose role went beyond the giving of battlefield relief, the original intent of the international Red Cross movement founded by Henry Dunant of Switzerland. Barton's society would serve America in peace as well as in war, especially in times of disaster and national calamity.

Victorian America was ready for a Red Cross. Civil war had ravaged the nation, and its people sought unity. The Indian wars were on the wane, telegraph lines hummed across the continent, and the golden spike had linked the railroads, bringing Americans closer together. It was also the age of "manifest destiny" as the government ended years of isolationism. All that was needed to spark support for a society was the persistence and charisma of Clara Barton.

Barton was a master of public relations technique. She wrote and lectured profusely, especially in the days following the Civil War, when she actively searched for soldiers missing in action. Those skills helped greatly as she lobbied for the United States government's support of the Geneva Convention, a treaty that guaranteed protection to the wounded. Without the government's endorsement, there could be no viable American Red Cross society.

The government's approval came in March 1882, but a confident Barton had already formed the American Association of the Red Cross on May 21, 1881. The tiny organization had even engaged in its first disaster relief activity, following the Michigan forest fires in the summer of that year. The stage was set for the kinds of work that would build Barton a loyal following over the years.

In the next twenty years, the Red Cross banner was raised over a string of disasters at home and abroad. Steamboats carrying supplies visited towns along the Mississippi in 1884 in the wake of devastating flooding; feeding stations and barracks were erected on the flood-scarred landscape of Johnstown in 1889; potato seeds and strawberry plants were distributed as well as clothing and food following the Sea

Islands and Galveston hurricanes of 1893 and 1900 respectively. Many disasters required extensive assistance from the small organization that depended on voluntary help and contributions to do its work.

Seeing in the American Red Cross a worldwide responsibility to ease suffering, Barton sent her volunteers overseas on behalf of relief groups that respected the implied neutrality of the organization. Although few in numbers, the relief workers carried out large-scale feeding and medical operations to aid famine-stricken Russians in 1892 and Armenian victims of Turkish massacres in 1896.

Barton's methods of running disaster operations were sometimes considered unorthodox. She was not a delegator. She insisted on personally supervising relief operations when possible, leaving the Red Cross headquarters leaderless until she returned. She also consistently kept "a stated sum of money" out of the bank and "upon momentary call," noting in 1904: "On more than one occasion it has been taken on Sunday, when every bank in the country was closed and charitable bodies were at their prayers. Even the relief of Johnstown was thus commenced." But the public loved her responsiveness, and generally chose to ignore occasional demands for better management.

A turning point came in 1898 with the Spanish-American War. The organization that had prided itself on quick response to fire, flood and famine found itself inadequate for war in Cuba and the Philippines. Barton's individual efforts received praise but the Red Cross as a whole remained small and operated haphazardly, drawing some criticism. Nevertheless, the Red Cross provided nurses, doctors and food, help that soldiers and refugees alike would have been deprived of had the organization failed to be on hand. President William McKinley, in his message to Congress in that year, praised the Red Cross for maintaining its high standards and "justifying the confidence and support" of the American people.

At home, Barton had lost control of the local Red Cross branches and auxiliaries. Their money financed her overseas operation and their personnel ran independent units in the Philippines. Particularly upsetting to her was their insistence on strict accountability of funds. In addition, little uniformity of services existed within the Red Cross as a whole. Even enactment of a congressional charter on June 6, 1900, following years of lobbying by Barton and others, failed to bring internal order despite clauses dealing with the use of the Red Cross name and emblem and organizational bylaws governing the formation of auxiliaries. It was clear by 1903 that centralized leadership was badly needed.

The first steps toward reform came from within. Ironically, the woman who was to lead the drive for reorganization was a volunteer whom Barton had successfully recommended for appointment to the Executive Committee in 1901. She was a socialite named Mabel Thorp Boardman, who was well educated, well organized and more important, influential. She was a woman whom Barton could neither intimidate nor ignore. Boardman believed that to survive in a changing America, the Red Cross had to start operating like a business. It didn't take her long to realize that Barton stood in the way of progress.

The Red Cross soon began to divide into two camps, those persons supporting

Barton and those favoring the ideas of Boardman, who wanted reorganization. Boardman led a strong minority faction but was unable to bring new people into the leadership structure because of bylaws changes enacted by the Barton majority. The majority even made Barton president for life. Events escalated rapidly, with Boardman using all her political influence. A protest was sent to President Theodore Roosevelt, and a petition was put before the Congress calling for an investigation into Red Cross affairs.

The days were bleak for Barton. Roosevelt withdrew official support from the organization in reaction to Boardman's protest over the bylaws changes, stunning Barton. The Red Cross Executive Committee retaliated by suspending Boardman from the Red Cross because of "her audacity," but nothing could be done to avert an investigation. In March 1904, a special committee composed of one senator, one House representative and the U.S. Adjutant General convened to hear testimony regarding general mismanagement and financial negligence, but its main purpose was to bring harmony to the Red Cross.

Barton's careless bookkeeping had caught up with her, and she admitted that an examination of the books "could mean trouble." She considered calling in her former accountant to prove "that I had a bookkeeper, the best in the country even if his records cannot be found."

The confrontation shocked America. Newspapers appeared to be evenly split between those chiding Boardman for her attack on the country's "grand old lady" and those calling for Barton's resignation for the good of the Red Cross. Everyone braced for a long-drawn-out battle, but victory came swiftly for Boardman. "The Committee had hardly been organized and certain evidence laid before it," wrote Boardman in 1931, "which was done behind closed doors at the request of the then officers of the Red Cross, when Miss Barton resigned." The date was May 3, 1904, the day that Barton was scheduled to testify. She never showed up, but neither did the key witness for the opposition. No more hearings were held, and no final committee report was ever issued. On May 14, 1904, Barton made her resignation public.

By late summer, the eighty-two-year-old Barton wrote in her diary: "The Red Cross has settled itself. I will resign even my membership, and when I can get out of my house and hands all that belongs to the new organization, it will be the same as if I had never known it." Within months she had formed the American First Aid Association, which competed with the Red Cross in the safety field between 1910 and 1912.

Long after her death in 1912, the public continued to see Clara Barton as the one truly representing the spirit of the Red Cross, a view that Boardman tried to discourage. When Barton was nominated for the Hall of Fame for Great Americans in New York City in 1940, Boardman urged the board of electors not to put too much stock in the legend surrounding Barton, alleging that "Miss Barton had an astonishing imagination that any experienced army officer would recognize in reading the quotations from her diary and other papers in her biography." But in 1976, a bid to place her name in the Hall was successful.

Adventuress or heroine? The truth may never be known. But Barton's two major achievements speak for themselves—the bringing about of the signing of the Geneva Convention treaty by the United States government and the establishment of a lasting Red Cross, officially chartered by the Congress in 1900 to meet the needs of the American people in times of calamity.

A group of wounded Union soldiers rest in the woods near Fredericksburg, Virginia, in May 1863. The Mathew B. Brady photograph was taken about the time that the Union was losing a major battle to the Confederacy at Chancellorsville. Clara Barton and women from both sides followed the battles, assisting the wounded. (National Archives)

"We drew a number of sanitary stores this afternoon," wrote a Union soldier in a letter home, "consisting of pickled onions, condensed milk, tomatoes, etc. I suppose of course, you know that by sanitary stores we mean provisions given us by the Sanitary Commission." The next day he added a postscript: "Back to our old diet—hard tack and coffee; like it very well indeed. Pound it and fry it like griddle cakes, fry it whole, make fish-balls of it; with coffee and sugar, who can complain?"

A Sanitary Commission unit poses for a photograph while awaiting marching orders. The maroon flag in front of the tent bears yellow letters reading "U.S. Sanitary Commission." The commission, a forerunner of the American Red Cross, was created by President Lincoln in 1861, mainly to cope with epidemics sweeping the Union army and threatening it with destruction. Its main job was to bring sanitary conditions to the camps and hospitals, where more men died from infected wounds and sickness than from actual combat. Various women's groups, and individuals such as Clara Barton, assisted the commission in its work. Charles S. Bowles, a member of the commission, represented the United States as an unofficial delegate to the Geneva Convention of 1864, arranged by the newly founded International Red Cross. The treaty that came out of the meeting assured the wounded protection in wartime, and France was the first nation to ratify the treaty.

The Civil War awakened the altruistic spirit of Clara Barton, a copier at the U.S. Patent Office in Washington, D.C. She took to the battlefields to give solace and aid to the wounded as a concerned American.

A rare photograph of three nurses who served during the Civil War. Various relief organizations and individuals helped nurse the wounded and ill behind the lines, including the Women's Central Association of Relief, whose petitions are said to have influenced President Lincoln's decision to create the U.S. Sanitary Commission.

Opposite:
"Miss Barton is what we call a strong hearted woman, not 'strong minded' in the invidious sense of the term," wrote a journalist in 1867. "She is noble in person, has a fine head and face, and is gifted with a rich voice which she modulates exquisitely." It is also said that she was superstitious, frugal, neurotic, prudish and extremely vain. She was referred to as "the Queen" and "Our Lady of the Cross" by some supporters, and as an "adventuress" or worse by her enemies. Born in North Oxford, Massachusetts, on Christmas Day in 1821, she rose from a small farm background to become a schoolteacher, government worker, Civil War nurse, women's prison superintendent and dedicated humanitarian. Although not a religious woman, late in life she endorsed the Christian Science movement and dabbled in spiritualism, consulting mediums and astrologers on occasion. This photograph was taken in 1866 by Mathew B. Brady.

6

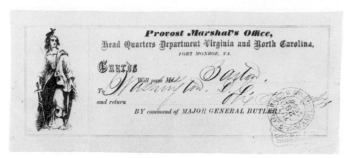

Passes used by Barton and her friends to cross the lines during the Civil War when she worked with the wounded.

The war over, Barton tidied up behind the holocaust, seeking the fate of missing soldiers and helping to establish at Andersonville, Georgia, site of the infamous Confederate prison, the first national cemetery.

General Ulysses S. Grant authorizes his officers to cooperate with Clara Barton in her efforts to locate missing soldiers following the end of the Civil War.

A woodcut from Harper's Weekly, *October 7, 1865, shows Barton raising the flag at the military cemetery at Andersonville, Georgia, site of an infamous Confederate war prison. Barton and two soldiers, one of them a former prisoner of war, were given authority by President Lincoln to search for missing men. They compiled a list of Union dead and compared their records with the grave markers at Andersonville. In this way they were able to identify and properly mark nearly 13,000 graves, making Andersonville the first national cemetery. (Library of Congress)*

The Civil War left its imprint on Barton. She carried explicit tales of battlefield woe to the people through lectures, drawing an emotional response, especially from veterans. "She had often been seen between the two contending armies," said one veteran in an 1867 letter to the *Cleveland Herald,* "administering to and caring for the wounded left behind. On one occasion, a wounded soldier whom she had raised up, was killed in her arms."

9

Veterans of the Civil War crowded Barton's lectures, where, as one New York reporter put it, "Perfect stillness prevailed, except when some noble utterance made applause irrepressible." She was one of the few who could put into words what the veterans had experienced. "We undertook to take a few notes of her discourse," said the reporter, "but soon gave up on the attempt as we became charmed and touched by her liquid elocution and pathetic story. She passed from one battlefield to another, graphically describing the shock of the combat, and the sad scenes which followed." It is reported that she received from $75 to $100 per lecture.

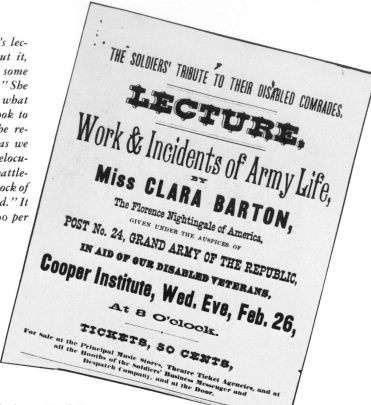

Traveling in Europe, Barton learned about Red Cross work. Her life changed inalterably following voluntary service with the Red Cross during the Franco-Prussian War.

Henry Dunant, a Swiss businessman whose compassion for the dying and wounded on a battlefield at Solferino, Italy, in 1859 led to the formation of a worldwide Red Cross movement. He wrote a book, A Memory of Solferino, publishing it in 1862, which turned the tragedy of one war into a victory for all humanity because it moved world leaders to press for an organization that could succor the wounded in wartime. The Red Cross was established in 1863 at Geneva, Switzerland, the year before the photograph was taken. A recipient of the first Nobel Peace Prize, in 1901, Dunant died in 1910 in a mountain village in Switzerland at age eighty-two, nearly penniless.

Clara Barton served as a Red Cross volunteer at Strasbourg, France, during the Franco-Prussian War of 1870–71. She wrote in 1900: "I had learned the use of the Red Cross, had learned to love, and respect it—to realize what misery and what lives it would have saved in our civil war if we had had it, and day by day, I pledged myself anew to its service in my own country if I could ever see it introduced there, and I promised the societies and the sovereigns of other nations to use every endeavor to bring it to the knowledge and the attention of the American government and of the American people."

Antoinette ("Kitty") Margo, Swiss by birth, was considered to be Barton's first Red Cross volunteer. She traveled with Barton to the front during the Franco-Prussian War and joined Barton's household in the United States in 1885, eventually leaving to teach French, her native tongue.

After several years in a sanitarium in Dansville, New York, Barton found herself well enough to begin actively seeking the formation of a Red Cross society in America. She took her case to the U.S. government in 1877 and was rebuffed on the most important step. The government refused to sign the Geneva Convention treaty of 1864, which ensured protection of the wounded in wartime. Five years later she would realize success.

The American Ambulance group, a forerunner of Clara Barton's society which flew the Red Cross flag, poses in Paris following the end of the 1870–71 Franco-Prussian War. Its leader, Dr. Joseph K. Riggs of Maryland (at center below the X), and three other members were awarded the Cross of the Legion of Honor by the French government for their outstanding assistance to the wounded during the siege of Paris. Riggs was later appointed by the U.S. government to oversee its distribution of money, food and seed to war victims.

Early attempts to plant the Red Cross banner in America failed, as the government studiously avoided signing the Geneva Convention treaty out of its fear of "entangling alliances."

Dr. Henry W. Bellows, president of the United States Sanitary Commission, sits for a portrait during the Civil War. Bellows tried to carry on with the work his commission did by setting up the American Association for the Relief of Misery on the Battlefield, which flew the Red Cross flag. The group collected funds for war relief during the Franco-Prussian War, but finally disbanded in 1872 when Bellows was unable to convince the U.S. government that America should be a party to the Geneva Convention. He wrote Barton in 1882, congratulating her on her own success and expressing his great disappointment that he had been unable to bring the government around.

Barton detected a change in the isolationist mood of the government in 1881 and established a Red Cross when it appeared certain the President would sign the Geneva treaty.

Years of lobbying to persuade the government that signing the Geneva Convention treaty was in the country's best interests finally bore fruit when President James A. Garfield asked his secretary of state in 1881 "to hear Miss Barton out." Garfield agreed that the treaty should be signed, but was assassinated before he could do it. President Chester Arthur followed through with the signing in 1882. "Thus, the spring of 1882 found us," wrote Barton, "a few people, tired and weak with five years of costly service, a treaty gained, with no fund, no war nor prospect of any, and no helpful connection with or acknowledgement by the government."

Clara Barton invites interested parties to attend the formation of the American Association of the Red Cross. She had decided to go ahead with the society when ratification of the 1864 Geneva Convention treaty by the U.S. government seemed certain. In 1893 the original articles of incorporation were revised, bringing about a name change. The organization started calling itself the American National Red Cross. The name remained unchanged until 1978, when the word "national" was dropped from general usage in an attempt to end the public misconception that the national and chapter sectors were separate entities.

"I have the gratifying privilege of informing you of the ratification by the Senate of the Geneva Convention," wrote E. G. Lapham to Barton from the Senate chambers on March 16, 1882, the same day the action was taken.

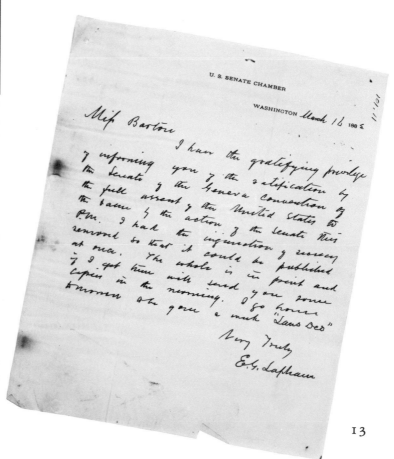

13

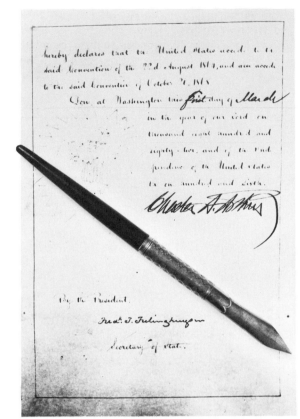

The pen of Chester A. Arthur rests upon a copy of the 1864 Geneva Convention, which he signed on March 1, 1882. The Senate ratified the treaty on March 16, making the United States the thirty-second country agreeing to protect the wounded during wartime. The act also signaled the end of America's fears of "entangling alliances." On July 26, 1882, President Arthur issued a proclamation notifying the American people of the nation's adherence to the treaty and acceptance of that ratification by the Swiss government.

Dansville, New York, around 1866. Barton made her first visit to the town in that year while on a lecture tour about her Civil War experiences. The first local Red Cross society in America was organized at the Lutheran Church (steeple with clock) on August 22, 1881. Rochester and Syracuse quickly followed suit, organizing local societies and cooperating with Dansville to provide contributions and supplies for Michigan forest fire victims.

Forest fires in Michigan drew the new Red Cross into its first relief effort, a limited action that started it on its way to becoming America's foremost disaster relief agency.

"Help or I perish!" A drawing from Leslies Weekly *(October 1881) of the famine situation that existed in the wake of the forest fires that ravaged parts of Michigan in the summer of 1881. Although only 125 persons were killed, thousands were left homeless, requiring extensive assistance from relief organizations, including the fledgling Red Cross. "Soon the news of 'Half the State of Michigan on Fire' called us to action on our own laws of civil relief," Barton wrote in 1904. New local societies from Dansville, Syracuse and Rochester, New York, raised funds and sent supplies to the stricken in the organization's first relief activity. Barton sent a field agent to survey the situation but did not go there herself.*

STRICKEN.
Michigan—"*Help, or I perish!*"

Dr. Julian B. Hubbell, sporting Dundrearies, surveyed the relief work in Michigan for Barton, becoming the organization's first field representative. He also directed some major relief activities for her, including famine relief in Russia in the early 1890s. A close friend until her death, Hubbell as a young man had asked Barton what he could do to help her start a Red Cross, and she advised him to become a doctor, which he did.

15

Rallying support during disasters was crucial to an organization that depended on volunteers and public contributions to do its work. Barton was a master at arousing the public's sympathy.

The steamboat Josh V. Throop *sits at the foot of Broadway in Cincinnati, Ohio, during the floods along the Ohio and Mississippi rivers in 1884. It was the first inland vessel in America to fly the Red Cross flag. "Boxes, bales, barrels, and bundles of clothing came in the name of the Red Cross from all over the Union," reported the* Daily Inter Ocean *on March 22, 1884. "Piles of blankets and quilts, stacks of boots and shoes, coats, vests, and trowsers, without end; underwear and hosiery, hats, caps, and bonnets, and every article of wearing apparel which poverty could suggest and generosity supply, could be found in the* Throop's *cargo."*

"The ladies and gentlemen of the Red Cross entered into the minutest details, and where necessity existed they were generous, but in the instances of hearty men, able bodied loafers who would not work when given an opportunity, and depended on the generosity of others for sustenance, it was promptly denied them by Miss Barton."

Daily Journal,
Evansville, Indiana, 1884

These youngsters initiated the first known Red Cross youth activity by raising over fifty dollars with a play in their town of Waterford, Pennsylvania. Clara Barton reportedly used the money to aid a large family that fell victim to the Ohio and Mississippi floods of 1884. "Sometime again when you want money to help you in your good work," they wrote, "call on the Little Six."

Famine threatened Russia in the late 1800s as it had done over the centuries. The public rallied behind an American Red Cross effort to provide corn and grain, giving evidence to the world of the great generosity of the people of the United States. In 1896, when the Turkish sword exercised genocide in Armenia, Barton personally led the Red Cross into its second overseas relief mission, one that saw it relying on camels and outpost stations to provide food and medical assistance to the Armenians.

Russians faced with starvation crowd a feeding station somewhere in Russia. Dr. Hubbell supervised the distribution of tons of wheat, corn, rye, and medical supplies in the first major relief effort by the American Red Cross overseas. Barton wrote to a contributor in April 1892 that she had been told by the Russian consul general that "corn and breadstuffs will render far more efficient aid than their value sent in money" and that all cash donations would be converted into foodstuffs. Of the 250 boxcars of corn sent by Iowa, she said the "splendid donation of corn will scarcely make more than one supper for this famishing nation."

Workers sort seed potatoes that will be used to restore inundated fields following the Sea Islands, South Carolina, hurricane which struck on August 27, 1893. The Red Cross fed more than thirty thousand homeless and starving persons and provided medical help and seeds in a rehabilitation project that went on for months.

Hurricanes challenged the early Red Cross. The organization would pick up in their wake for decades to come.

Relief workers ponder the day's tasks in the private office and stenographer's room at Red Cross headquarters in Beaufort, South Carolina. Spanish moss hangs from the walls and pine cones decorate the table amid bundles of letters, books and a carefully placed publication (foreground) bearing the likeness of Clara Barton. The woman sits at a typewriter.

THE DESTRUCTION OF GALVESTON.
DRAWN BY G. W. PETERS FROM TELEGRAPHIC REPORTS.

Victims of the Galveston tidal waves cling to debris in this 1900 drawing by G. W. Peters which was based on telegraphic reports. It was the most devastating disaster to require Red Cross assistance up to that time. The tidal waves ripped away buildings and drowned 15 percent of the population. For weeks on end, fires burned day and night as the city tried to get rid of debris and the thousands of corpses and animal carcasses that made the streets impassable. "That peculiar smell of burning flesh," wrote Barton, "so sickening at first, became horribly familiar within the next two months, when we lived in it and breathed it, day after day."

The hurricane and tidal waves that began hitting Galveston, Texas, on September 8, 1900, left 6,000 dead. The Red Cross spent $120,000 on relief, including the purchase of 1.5 million strawberry plants to help the many farmers in their recovery. This was the last time that Clara Barton, then seventy-eight years old, actively participated in a disaster relief project.

Galveston, Texas, October 7, 1900.

APPEAL FOR THE HOMELESS OF GALVESTON.

Does the evidence here portrayed bring to you a thought of the distressing need of Galveston's homeless survivors? Do you not feel that it is your duty to contribute your portion to the worthy work of procuring shelter and household goods for those who are now without shelter? Do you realize that a small sum from each sympathizer will aggregate an amount sufficient to meet this great and pressing need? All money should be remitted to

MISS CLARA BARTON, President,
American National Red Cross, Galveston, Texas.

No. 43 Remarks— *During the storm*

Location *East 2* for 25 cts.

W. A. GREEN, Galveston, Texas.

19

The Red Cross headquarters at 25th Street and Strand in Galveston, jointly shared with the New York World, which "had opened a subscription for the relief of Galveston, and would send all supplies and money received to the Red Cross." Joining with the Salvation Army and other groups, Barton and her volunteers set up a warehouse for the distribution of clothing, which included some one million donated shirtwaists and another million "Mother Hubbard" wrappers—loose-fitting dresses—which Barton despised. "There were enough," she recalled, "to disfigure every female in Southern Texas." When the Red Cross work of feeding and clothing the victims was finished, Barton moved her operation to the Houston area, where more victims were to be found.

Barton and Susan B. Anthony were among the distinguished leaders called upon to rally support for woman suffrage around 1888. Although Barton didn't spend a great deal of time lobbying for women's rights, Anthony occasionally called on her for support. Barton joined Anthony at a suffragette meeting in Washington in 1904. She noted in her diary, February 17: "Miss Anthony desired me to speak. I utterly declined. She then drew me beside her to the front of the stage and stood there with her arm about me while she told the audience that I was at the first Suffrage Meeting in Washington in 1869. That later I sent out my call to the soldiers to stand by women as I had stood by them. . . ."

Disaster relief projects multiplied over the years. In addition to the larger ones, the Red Cross attended to famine in Texas, cyclones in Illinois and yellow fever epidemics in Florida. With all the work, Barton could only wonder in 1888, "with a mingled national and personal sense of indignation, why our American Red Cross is not as rich and great as in other nations?"

20

Camp Perry, a yellow fever quarantine station near Jacksonville, Florida, where "objectionable characters," including wayward women posing as Red Cross nurses, were sent during epidemics in 1888. Barton was outraged when she learned that women passing themselves off as nurses were sullying the reputations of legitimate Red Cross workers. A number of nurses, most of them from the New Orleans branch of the Red Cross, were operating out of a hospital at Jacksonville. The chief physician there brought in a highly respected nurse from a New York hospital to take charge. She was Jane Delano, future chairman of the Red Cross Nursing Service, who was not yet connected with the organization. "Our little part of the relief of that misfortune was estimated at fifteen-thousand dollars," said Barton, "and only those relieved were more grateful than we."

Barton had involved the Red Cross in services beyond the field of disaster by 1888, using willing volunteers.

A national drill competition on the Mall at the Washington Monument gave the Red Cross a chance to demonstrate its first-aid skills in 1886. Clara Barton reported that the Red Cross hospital (lower right corner) "treated accident victims, numerous illnesses, and sunstroke, and not one of our patients went home in a box." (Library of Congress)

The South Fork Dam at Johnstown, Pennsylvania, burst on May 31, 1889, killing more than 2,000 persons. The first train to reach the scene carried Red Cross workers led by Barton. They spent five months rehabilitating the population, directly assisting 25,000 people.

Debris-strewn Johnstown, Pennsylvania, following the collapse of the South Fork Dam near the Conemaugh River. Barton and her volunteers arrived within forty-eight hours to find "four thousand dead in the river beds, twenty thousand foodless but for the Pittsburgh bread rations, and a cold rain which continued unbroken by sunshine for forty days." The Red Cross immediately set up feeding stations and provided unprecedented medical care through the nurses of the Philadelphia Red Cross Society.

The famous Johnstown flood of 1889 provided the Red Cross with a major test of its ability to deal with a large-scale catastrophe of the manmade variety.

There were some complaints about the Red Cross actions at Johnstown. David Beale, in his 1890 book, *Through the Johnstown Flood,* noted that when the Red Cross began providing mass relief, it often helped "the lazy and shiftless to the neglect of the worthy and needy." The author suggested that the organization should have stuck to providing medical care to avoid the problem, but admitted that generally the society "did a great deal of good."

One of the six Red Cross buildings that housed victims of the flood. The "Red Cross Hotels" were run like hotels, but at no cost to the tenants. Three thousand smaller houses were built by the city and the Red Cross furnished them from donations sent by big businesses around the country. The disaster marked the first time the organization had set up mass shelters. When the operation ended in late October, the Red Cross had its warehouse and hotels torn down. Their lumber was distributed to residents of Johnstown until local lumber dealers protested. Much of it was then sent to Washington.

The battleship Maine *enters Havana harbor on January 25, 1898. On February 15, it exploded there, taking 260 Americans to the bottom and triggering the Spanish-American War. Clara Barton and her assistants were working with Cuban insurrectionists imprisoned by Spain when the incident occurred, and she had dined aboard the vessel just two days earlier. Barton returned home shortly before the U.S. government declared war on Spain in late April of 1898. (National Archives)*

Barton, already working with starving *reconcentrados* in Cuba, made the Red Cross available to the U.S. military following America's declaration of war on Spain in April 1898. President McKinley expressed America's gratitude for the feeding of U.S. troops and the giving of medical aid to the wounded.

Clara Barton (seated at center in dark clothes) waits with her entourage for U.S. Navy permission to sail the State of Texas *to blockaded Cuba, where war raged. They remained at Tampa and Key West, Florida, for two frustrating months, finally departing on June 20, 1898. The navy had feared the Spanish would capture the supplies.*

23

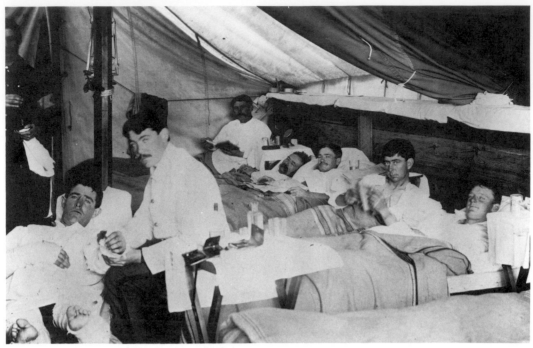

Medical corpsmen dress wounds and look after fever victims of the U.S. Third Cavalry at Fort McKenzie, Georgia, in 1898. Conditions at many camps left much to be desired, especially in Florida and Cuba, where yellow fever and typhoid fever were rampant. A Red Cross nurse waiting in Tampa for a ship to take her to Cuba reported that "desperately sick fever patients, United States soldiers on United States soil, were lying on cots between heavy military blankets, no sheets, no pillows, no towels, no mosquito netting although they were being tormented beyond words by mosquitoes, flies and sand fleas." Army medical officers admitted that at times their operation would have broken down completely without help from the Red Cross. (National Archives)

An ambulance driver and a horseback rider wait outside the office of the American Red Cross at Camp Thomas, Georgia, during the Spanish-American War. The first known Red Cross activity of a nonmedical type for soldiers reportedly occurred at Fort McPherson, Georgia, where a field agent carried on a communications service, handling inquiries from a few families.

The State of Texas *steams toward Cuban waters following the lifting of the U.S. blockade, with Clara Barton and her party aboard. The Red Cross set up field kitchens in Santiago, feeding about fifty thousand refugees in the first five days from supplies carried aboard the ship.*

Information for recruited nurses. Early in the war, the U.S. surgeon general allowed only men to work with battlefield casualties, but public opinion and the demonstrated competence of women nurses during the yellow fever epidemics of 1888 in Florida changed his mind. Barton and others traveled to various hospitals to find recruits, who were screened and contracted to the army, working for approximately thirty dollars monthly.

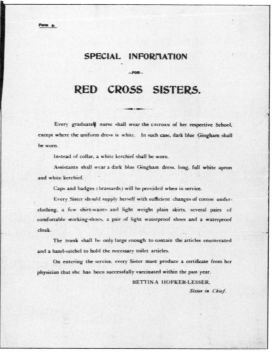

Interior of an upper-deck ward aboard the hospital ship Relief *in Cuban waters. Red Cross nurses served aboard such U.S. Navy ships during the Spanish-American War. The man wearing the brassard with the red cross on it was probably an army or a navy medical corpsman. A Red Cross nurse is partially visible to the left of the pillar. (Armed Forces Institute of Pathology)*

Red Cross nurses en route to Cuba, where in 1898 the American army battled yellow fever, typhoid and the Spanish troops. A nurse aboard the S.S. Lampasas told how their ship came alongside another ship and took aboard about eighty sick soldiers, "a pitiful line of staggering, reeling men dragging themselves along with parched lips and glassy, staring eyes. Many of course had to be carried on. They all wore the regulation blue flannel shirt and heavy cloth uniform although burning with fever under a hot July sun in the tropics."

Soldiers of the Seventh Infantry in their trenches on San Juan Hill in July 1898. Colonel Teddy Roosevelt gained fame, which helped him win the presidency, when he led his Rough Riders in a charge up the hill. (National Archives)

Clara Barton at the International Conference of the Red Cross in St. Petersburg, Russia, on June 2, 1902, with Red Cross delegate B. F. Tillinghast (left), editor of the Davenport, Iowa, Democrat, and Russian Admiral N. Kazakoff. Barton was decorated at the conference for Red Cross help given during the great Russian famine of 1892.

This article and drawing appeared in the New York World *on March 11, 1900.*

Clever Trained Elephants That Act as Red Cross Nurses.

THE elephant's role as a Red Cross nurse is a novel one. His usefulness in this sphere, however, will be seen by the pictures, which are taken from snapshots made of a number of these four-footed nurses engaged in their duties of mercy.

The trainer of these docile beasts is Henry Mooney, who has spent years in India studying his pets. The drama in which they are actors is a mock battle.

In their Red Cross exercises one huge elephant falls to the ground in the fray and lies as if dead. The trainer does the same, whereupon the other animals carry off his body on their trunks. The baby elephant shown in the illustration has been taught to wield a white flag of truce, trumpeting with rage when the enemy refuses to recognize his signal and continues firing.

These intelligent four-footed Florence Nightingales came from Hyderabad and were secured by their owner for about $870 each. Their ages, with the exception of the baby, vary from seven to thirteen years, and their average weight is 4,000 pounds.

27

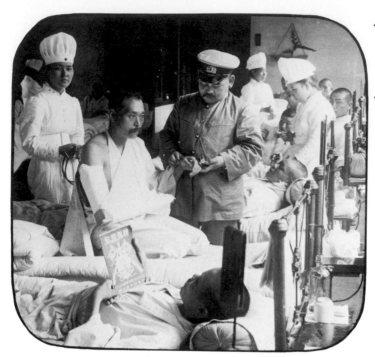

Japanese Red Cross doctors and nurses look after the wounded at the Army Reserve Hospital in Hiroshima. Only male nurses attended the wounded at the front during the Russo-Japanese War, which the Russians lost. The Red Cross in Japan was highly advanced, having over $4 million in its treasury, as opposed to the $124 in Barton's coffers at the end of 1903. A Philadelphia newspaper reported in 1903 that the Japanese Red Cross had an annual income of $1 million from membership dues and a force of 2,500 nurses ready for active service when needed, dwarfing the American Red Cross.

A Red Cross first-aid kit in 1903 made of wood, with its handy chart and a textbook. The First Aid Department of the Red Cross, directed by Englishman Edward Howe, planned to start ambulance brigades and teach first aid to the public. A treatment for snakebite recommended cleansing of the wound by suction and washing, calling for a doctor and giving "Brandy or Whiskey in large quantities."

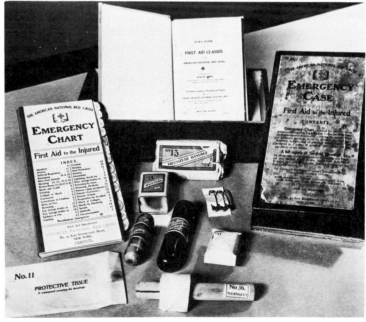

A scroll of thanks sent to Barton in 1904 after she had already resigned from the Red Cross. Count Matsukata, head of the Japanese Red Cross Society, informed her belatedly that her offer to provide nurses during the Russo-Japanese War of 1904–5 was received with gratitude but that their presence was not needed. Against Barton's wishes, the Philadelphia Red Cross Society defiantly sent nurses to the Japanese Army Reserve Hospital in Hiroshima to work with the incoming wounded.

The progressive mood sweeping America touched the venerable Red Cross in 1903 from within, bringing bitterly contested reform to the organization. The days of the Barton regime were nearly at an end.

Mabel Boardman brought reform to the Red Cross after years of its domination by Clara Barton. Boardman's direct involvement with the Barton regime first came when she was selected as one of fifty incorporators under the 1900 charter of the Red Cross. She was a woman "sought after at once in society and in philanthropy, to be at the same time distinctively intellectual and yet nothing of a bluestocking," said The American Magazine *in 1910. "And Miss Boardman is just entering her prime—a woman of more than medium height, rather slender, with a liking for modish gowns and the details of the business of the Red Cross."*

THE NEW CRUSADER.

The cartoon gibes at President Roosevelt for withdrawing official recognition from the Red Cross following the bylaws changes and at Barton's "haughty" letter to him protesting his action. "Clara Barton should master the difficult art of knowing when not to write letters," editorialized the Post *in Hartford, Connecticut, in an obvious dig at her penchant for writing voluminously.*

CLARA BARTON HITTING BACK

Suspends 22 Prominent Persons from Red Cross.

ROOSEVELT'S SISTER ONE

Defiant Minority Ordered to Appear and Explain Why All Should Not Be Ejected.

From the Regular Correspondent of The Press.

WASHINGTON, April 7.—Red Cross factionalism and individual jealousness in that organization were carried another step further to-day, when a statement was received here informing the Washington members, who had planned to have Clara Barton retire from the presidency, that they had been suspended by the Executive Committee which met in New York. Walter P. Phillips, chairman of the Executive Committee, and one of Miss Barton's adherents, sent this interesting notice here:

"The American National Red Cross at a meeting of the Executive Committee, held in this city yesterday suspended from mem-

"Every time Theodore opens his mouth he puts his foot in it," said the *Times* of Shreveport, Louisiana, in a February 26, 1904, editorial. "His latest mistake was to sever his connection with the Red Cross society. The American people think a great deal of that organization."

30

Clara Barton's home in Glen Echo, Maryland, near Washington, as it looked in 1904. Barton (second from left) had it built about 1891 with wood bought for building shelters following the Johnstown flood. It was first used as a warehouse, its hollowed-out walls in the hallway and movable partitions providing space for storage of Red Cross supplies. She had it modified in 1897, for use as living quarters and a headquarters. The house is run by the National Park Service and is open to visitors.

Mrs. John Logan, Barton's vice-president, registered a public protest against Theodore Roosevelt following the death of the Red Cross founder, which was read into the Congressional Record on June 18, 1912. In a eulogy on Barton's behalf, Congressman William P. Borland noted the "strong indignation" of Logan, widow of General John Logan, which was carried in a newspaper article. She said that Barton had "died of a broken heart, hounded by her enemies." And she followed up by saying: "The hand of Theodore Roosevelt, then President of the United States, drove the first nail into the cross of distrust and suspicion against Miss Barton."

2. The Age of Innocence

The reorganization of the American Red Cross in 1905 matches the intense progressiveness of the times. Reform is afoot in the nation and in the Red Cross. As the country bursts out of the Victorian age, the organization moves toward the greatest unity and solidarity of purpose it has ever known and again enjoys the support of Teddy Roosevelt. The reformer Mabel Boardman succeeds in those areas where Clara Barton failed.

Armed with a new federal charter that improved the organization's relationship with the government, Boardman and a few supporters opened a Red Cross office in Washington, D.C., hardly knowing what to do. They began by settling internal affairs. They paid bills, curtailed disaster relief work due to lack of funds, and sought financial backing. The congressional charter of 1905 was welcome, but it put additional pressure on the nearly defunct national Red Cross. While conferring semiofficial status, it also added new responsibilities—financial accountability and the furnishing of a "medium of communication between the people of the United States and their Army and Navy." Boardman and her administration quickly realized that to survive, the Red Cross would have to win the support of the American people through effective action.

On the morning of April 18, 1906, at 5:12 A.M., the city of San Francisco heaved and buckled as an earthquake shook it to pieces. Fires raged. Nearly five hundred persons died and hundreds more were injured. Tens of thousands were made homeless in a matter of minutes. But the agony of the quake revealed the great potential of the Red Cross by forcing the organization into action. Refusing to accept Boardman's protests that the Red Cross was ill equipped to handle a relief operation of that magnitude, President Roosevelt ordered the organization to assist the army and other agencies. The result was a commendable showing that emboldened the organization's approach in the coming years.

The Red Cross grew more aggressive. No longer content to wait for disasters to happen, it became teacher and rescuer, fund raiser and benefactor, organizer and social conscience. New Red Cross branches were established and existing ones were pulled under one administrative umbrella, ending the complete local autonomy that once threatened internal unity. Eventually, plans were made for the building of a permanent headquarters in Washington, helping the Red Cross to shed its transient look and telling the people it would be around for a long time.

The period also saw the emergence of colorful personalities who would strongly influence the organization's work while providing the public with identifiable figures. One was Jane Delano, whose appointment in 1909 led to a true nursing service which spearheaded a relentless attack on communicable diseases both in the towns and on the farms. Another was Commodore Wilbert E. Longfellow, a former newspaperman, whose love of swimming inspired him to try to reverse the nation's alarming drowning rate. He succeeded in making the Red Cross the undisputed master of water safety instruction.

There were others who contributed greatly to the early growth of Red Cross services in those exploratory years, including Major Charles Lynch, initial head of the first-aid program, and Ernest Bicknell, first national director of relief, who had proved himself during the San Francisco earthquake. Even Boardman assumed an unaccustomed role, taking to the road to push for the burgeoning first-aid program, and never allowing mine and factory owners to forget that they had a duty to their employees and their country where safety was concerned.

By 1914, the Red Cross had established viable patterns of national service. Inroads had been made into the public health and safety areas. Red Cross Christmas Seals had successfully appeared in the battle against the "Great White Plague," tuberculosis. And hands had been joined with other social agencies and industry to meet America's future needs. In an operation that was to continue off and on until 1917, Red Cross relief personnel were busy along the Texas border, feeding, medically treating, and sheltering tens of thousands of refugees caught up in the Mexican civil war. Limited as it was, the activity was a portent of what lay ahead in war-threatened Europe.

The period ended with the organization still seeking greater involvement of the public in its work, especially in terms of membership. But the reorganization had succeeded against great odds, and the Red Cross had developed into a potential social force that needed only World War I to ignite its true power. And through it all, there had been the firm leadership of Mabel Boardman, the no-nonsense volunteer, who was, as Bicknell once put it, "the chief. Make no mistake about that."

Public apathy plagued the reorganized Red Cross. Volunteers were few and contributions skimpy. Mabel Boardman often used her own funds in the early years just to keep the Red Cross office running. "Few were interested," she would say one day in retrospect; "war was improbable in the public estimation, and disasters could be cared for when they occurred."

Volunteer leader Mabel Boardman works at a desk in the one room that made up Red Cross headquarters in the State-War-Navy Building next to the White House in 1910. Some wondered if the Red Cross could survive in the hard days following Clara Barton's resignation. At a banquet commemorating the fiftieth anniversary of the Red Cross in 1931, Boardman remembered that in 1905, "A local habitation was necessary, and a small room was rented in a business building, and there the faithful secretary, Mr. Charles L. Magee, and myself, with an occasional visit from the chairman of the Central Committee, Admiral Van Reypen, started to work. On what? We hardly knew." In the photograph, Magee works to the far right while an assistant, Francis Muhall, reads at center.

Prior to the opening of the Panama Canal, the American Red Cross established, in January 1909, a Canal Zone branch to provide financial assistance in emergency situations to workers and their families and to give advice "to the wayward." Shortly after, it began concentrating on the teaching of first aid to the people who operated the canal. It would continue its work with the military and others for the next seventy years. In 1979, the Canal Zone Chapter closed its doors for good as the United States turned over the waterway to the Panamanians.

On November 1, 1909, the Red Cross Executive Committee established "chapters" as opposed to independent "societies," "associations," and the like. The chapters reported directly to national headquarters for administrative purposes, so that their activities could be coordinated and the Red Cross could operate as one united force.

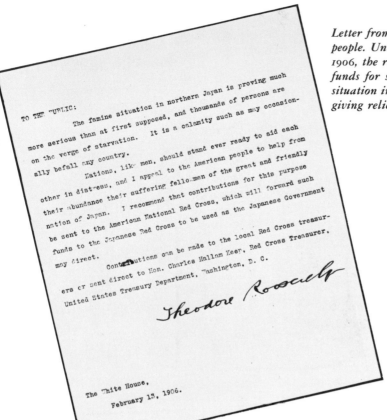

Letter from President Roosevelt to the American people. Until the earthquake in San Francisco in 1906, the reorganized Red Cross mainly collected funds for such activities as relieving the famine situation in Japan, but it played no active role in giving relief.

The earthquake reduced San Francisco to rubble, leaving some 250,000 persons homeless and presenting the Red Cross with the "supreme test and the supreme opportunity," as Boardman recalled years later.

Crowds line up on Van Ness Avenue to pick up relief supplies from the Red Cross and other charitable groups under its supervision. All funds were turned over to the Red Cross for distribution. The moneys, according to the 1910 annual report to Congress, gave the residents of San Francisco "not only sustenance, but that courage, fortitude, and enterprise which enabled them, with surprising rapidity, to rehabilitate themselves and their city. It was the constant aim of the committee to encourage self-reliance, and not by outright gift, to induce pauperization."

President Roosevelt appealed to the nation for contributions and asked that the public send them to the Red Cross, "as the only organization chartered and authorized by Congress to act at times of great national calamity." The Red Cross worked closely with the army and formed a corporation with citizens' relief groups called The San Francisco Relief and Red Cross Funds, a Corporation. The corporation distributed contributions, government moneys, and supplies.

A Red Cross worker treats a man injured in the fire following the San Francisco earthquake in 1906, but appears more interested in the camera.

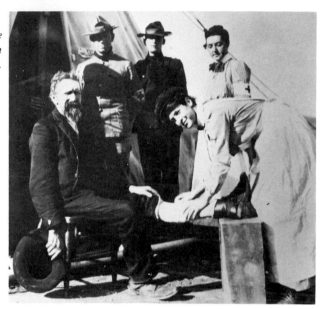

Homeless men wait for a meal in San Francisco. Cooking in the available homes was prohibited to prevent a fresh outbreak of fire. The Red Cross and the Bureau of Relief Stations jointly provided police protection, water and fuel, sites for the stations, and meal tickets, while outside contractors did the cooking.

Headquarters of the American Red Cross during the 1906 earthquake in San Francisco.

A Japanese dentist (left) retrieves his dental chair out of the ashes of his former office.

One of the many camps used to shelter the homeless in San Francisco. The Red Cross found it difficult to control the sanitary and moral conditions of the camps and worried about "the inclination of many to live lives of idleness while support may be obtained from relief funds, thereby creating a future pauper class."

Orphaned children of some 256 miners entombed in a coal mine at Cherry, Illinois, on November 13, 1909. The final death toll reached nearly 260 as would-be rescuers were trapped in a fire on the second level of the mine. Earlier that year, Boardman wrote in the Red Cross Magazine: *"Statistics show that in our mines alone over seven men are killed a day and nearly twenty injured." The Red Cross established a pension fund for the widows and orphans from contributions that came from individuals, labor unions and the Illinois legislature. The fund influenced the passage of workmen's compensation laws in many states, which forced industries to take more responsibility for the welfare of their employees.*

38

The Red Cross entered a busy period in 1911 that continued for three years. The chapters and national headquarters coped with forty-four disasters, sixteen of them overseas. Most prominent of the disaster operations were the Triangle Waist Factory fire in New York in 1911, in which 145 persons died, and the wreck of the "unsinkable" S.S. *Titanic,* in which 1,571 were killed the following year. In both instances, the bulk of Red Cross financial assistance went to the families of the deceased, whether living in the United States or abroad.

The Red Cross pioneered between 1906 and 1914, establishing services in nursing, first aid, and water safety, and developing the use of Christmas Seals to fund its battle on tuberculosis.

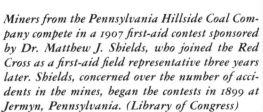

Between 1909 and 1912, railroad and streetcar safety became a Red Cross priority. "On the principle that an ounce of prevention is worth a pound of cure," said Boardman in December 1909, "over sixty thousand posters on which are printed precautions against accidents have been given on their request to the railroads of the country, to be posted in their stations." Eventually, about 100,-000 were distributed, including smaller ones for trolley cars.

Miners from the Pennsylvania Hillside Coal Company compete in a 1907 first-aid contest sponsored by Dr. Matthew J. Shields, who joined the Red Cross as a first-aid field representative three years later. Shields, concerned over the number of accidents in the mines, began the contests in 1899 at Jermyn, Pennsylvania. (Library of Congress)

A pattern of helping Americans help themselves developed that would continue for the next seventy-five years. Instead of waiting for the alarm to sound, the Red Cross began trying to teach Americans how to avoid certain calamities through safety awareness and health care practices.

The Pullman first-aid car. Instructors in 1911 give a class to railroad workers in front of "old Number One," most famous of the cars donated to the Red Cross by the Pullman Company. It was pulled out of service at the beginning of World War I, but resumed its runs along the nation's railroads in 1923 under the directorship of Dr. Matthew Shields. It reached an estimated one million people before being retired in 1929. The car, built of wood in 1881 and repaired numerous times, prompted Shields to say, "The car is a contradiction to what the men on the car are teaching —safety and first aid."

Railroad men learn to apply a bandage to a suspected broken arm in 1910.

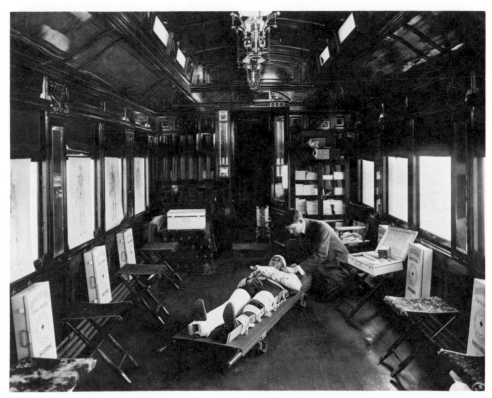

Interior of first-aid car. Instruction Car Number One was equipped with a lecture room, a kitchen, an office, and sleeping quarters for the personnel, who usually included two physicians and a "Chinese cook." The Red Cross had three such cars by 1916, but one was destroyed in a train wreck in that year. By the time America entered the war in 1917, it had several more, but they were all turned over to the Public Health Service for use by the military.

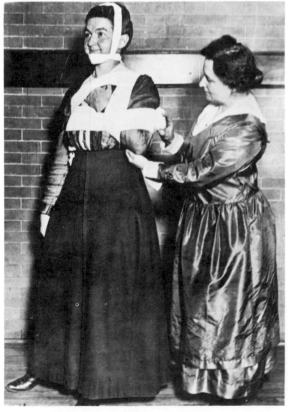

An elaborate bandage becomes part of a young woman's ensemble. Clara Barton's first-aid program was discontinued as impractical following the reorganization of the Red Cross. In 1910, the program was revived as the First Aid Department. The Red Cross soon joined with the YMCA to jointly sponsor first-aid classes that emphasized industrial safety.

"Can you tell me who coined the term 'Safety First'?" asked Charles Fay, safety director at the Davis Coal and Coke Company of Cumberland, Maryland, in a 1916 letter to Mabel Boardman. Boardman replied: "Probably no one has had more to do with the use of that term and safety movement among miners than the late Dr. J. A. Holmes, of the Bureau of Mines, Washington, D.C." She added: "Mr. Richards, of the Chicago and Northwestern Railroad, also claims to be the author of the slogan."

An early fund-raising poster.

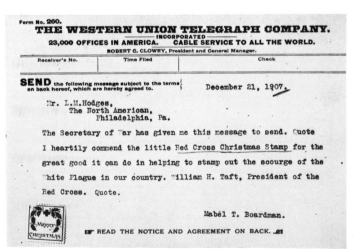

Telegram sent to the North American *newspaper in Philadelphia for publicity purposes.*

THE CHALLENGE

A CARTOON APPEARING IN THE PHILADELPHIA "LEDGER," LAST NOVEMBER.

Christmas Seals finance the battle against tuberculosis. The 1910 Annual Report noted that the Red Cross ordered eighty million of them printed for sale at one cent each, the profits to be turned over to the National Association for the Study and Prevention of Tuberculosis.

Scene in the Wilmington, Delaware, post office on December 7, 1907. Emily P. Bissell, secretary of the Delaware branch of the American Red Cross, is buying the first Christmas Seal sold in the United States from Red Cross worker Lillie Ray. The Red Cross turned the activity over to the National Tuberculosis Association in 1919. All the moneys collected were used solely for anti-TB activities and the printing of the seals.

THE
PUBLIC HEALTH NURSE

She Answers Humanity's Call

Your Red Cross Membership makes her work possible

*"To her district she is nurse, mother, sister, teacher and fairy-godmother,"
boasts a brochure of the day in describing a rural nurse. "In a week she
attends the sick, instructs mothers, gives the school children lessons in hygiene,
organizes health committees and clubs, brings clean-up and public-welfare
campaigns to the country, apparently carrying in her bag a new lease of life
for all to whom it opens." Rural Nursing, initiated in 1912, became Town
and Country Nursing the following year and remained a popular Red Cross
service.*

The reorganized Red Cross lacked the romance of Barton's day during its first few years, but the problem
solved itself as colorful personalities joined in and put
their imaginations to work on the problems of America.

44

Jane Delano in full uniform as chairman of the Red Cross Nursing Service. She resigned her position as superintendant of the Army Nurse Corps in 1912 in order to serve the Red Cross without pay on a full-time basis. "My only object in resigning is that I may have the time to devote to the development and maintenance of an efficient reserve of Red Cross nurses for the service of the Army," she stated in a letter to the surgeon general.

The Red Cross Nursing Service grew stronger and in 1912 Jane Delano made a true commitment to the organization that she had helped over the years. "I would rather live on a crust and serve the Red Cross," she said in resigning from the Army Nurse Corps, "than do anything else in the world."

"A knowledge of driving and riding horses, and sometimes the use of a bicycle, is necessary in some communities," said a brochure recruiting Town and Country Nurses in 1914. Visiting nurses, who provided continuous service in small towns and rural districts across the country, were expected to take an interest in the general welfare of patients and to try to improve the environment of the families they visited.

A Red Cross public health nurse proudly poses with her Model T Ford before setting out on her rounds. The Town and Country Nursing Service became the Bureau of Public Health Nursing in May 1918. In order to overcome a shortage of nurses trained in public health, the Red Cross set up a scholarship fund in 1919 to prepare graduate nurses for a career in the field.

The Red-Cross Girl

A VOLUME OF FICTION

=== By ===

Richard Harding Davis

Illustrated

$1.25

Net

By Mail

$1.35

—

Charles

Scribner's

Sons

Fifth Avenue, New York

"Trouble came to him wearing the blue cambric uniform of a nursing sister," said Davis's about-to-be-smitten newspaper reporter in a 1912 story, "with a red cross on her arm, with a white collar turned down, white cuffs turned back, and a tiny black velvet bonnet. A bow of white lawn chucked her impudently under the chin. She had hair like goldenrod and eyes as blue as flax, and a complexion of such health and cleanliness and dewiness as blooms only on trained nurses."

Ernest Percy Bicknell, first national director of Red Cross relief, set disaster assistance patterns that were copied by the government because of their effectiveness. The former Indianapolis newspaperman maintained that the energy of the Red Cross should be saved "for large and important undertakings" and "must not interfere with good work which is being accomplished by any other agency and must be so strong that no other agency will be tempted to invade our field." Bicknell became associated with the Red Cross during the San Francisco earthquake. Boardman, who appointed him in 1906, said years later: "The call had come. The Red Cross volunteered, and its existence became known to the people of the United States. That cloud had a silver lining, and that silver lining was Colonel Ernest P. Bicknell. He came to the Red Cross and he has remained a silver lining for many another cloud." Bicknell died in September 1935 at the age of seventy-three, having eventually risen to vice-chairman of the organization.

Refugees, mainly French-Canadian workers, lived here for weeks following a fire that razed the tenement and industrial half of Salem, Massachusetts, June 25, 1914, in the greatest holocaust since San Francisco.

The Red Cross guidelines for providing relief in disasters were outlined by Bicknell: "Our relief fund is not an insurance fund. The amount of a family's losses is not an index to the amount which may be afforded it. The only guide for us is the extent of each family's needs and its ability to re-establish itself."

Horses swim against floodwaters inundating the streets of Dayton, Ohio, March 13, 1913. Nearly two thirds of the city was affected. The flooding in the Ohio Valley cost 500 lives and caused millions of dollars in damages, setting the Red Cross in action. The organization sent in 270 nurses and rapidly activated about 20 relief groups and social agencies holding "institutional membership" in the Red Cross. Working closely with them, the Red Cross established relief units in 43 communities, handling some 300,000 flood victims in the initial stages. The Red Cross dropped the use of institutional members in 1921 when it became obvious that outside social workers did not have time for lengthy relief operations. (Library of Congress)

U.S. soldiers arrive in Dayton to protect the city from looting and to maintain order, bringing with them wagons full of supplies for the flood victims.

A curfew sign is posted to cut down on the incidence of looting.

To the Citizens of Dayton:

CURFEW

will be sounded at 6:00 p. m. by the church bells. All citizens must keep off the streets from that time until 5:00 a. m.

GEO. H. WOOD,
Brig.-Gen. Com.

The first Red Cross Life Saving Corps Station, built in 1914 at Pablo Beach, Florida, now known as Jacksonville Beach. Taken in 1917, the photograph shows two men trained in surf rescue and a woman first-aid attendant.

Commodore Wilbert E. Longfellow, "the amiable whale," gives a demonstration of a rescue technique in a canal. On February 1, 1914, the Red Cross started a service devoted to "water first aid," with the newly acquired Longfellow as its head. The service was officially known as the Life Saving Corps of the American National Red Cross. Longfellow traveled round the country, the lone field representative for the corps for years, teaching policemen, boy scouts and YMCA groups, and visiting colleges and universities. Although the Life Saving Corps was part of the First Aid Department, it was years before Longfellow earned a first aid certificate because the doctors teaching first aid "were so busy with their program and I with mine that our paths seldom crossed."

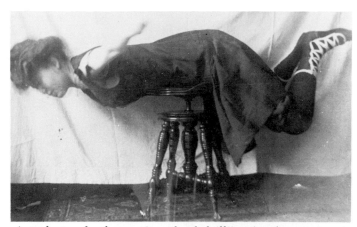

A student ardently practices "land drill" swimming movements, circa 1900. Commodore Longfellow believed swimming should be taught in the water.

The "Marble Palace" begins to take shape in 1915. The large columns in the foreground were moved around on mule-drawn carts. Earlier that year, at the groundbreaking ceremonies, former U.S. President William H. Taft, the principal speaker, spoke somewhat prophetically when he noted that the dedication was "sadly, but fitly timed. We are in the greatest war in history. The sacrifices we are to make we cannot realize. The work of the women of the United States was never more important." The building was dedicated to the memory of the "heroic women of the Civil War."

The national headquarters of the American Red Cross at Seventeenth and D streets, N.W., Washington, D.C., a national landmark. It was completed in 1917. The total cost was $800,000, half of it paid by congressional appropriation, the rest by private subscribers—James A. Scrymser, Mrs. Russell Sage, Mrs. E. H. Harriman and the Rockefeller Foundation. The stained-glass windows in the upstairs Board of Governors Hall were the work of Louis C. Tiffany's studio in New York. They were donated by two post–Civil War groups, the United Daughters of the Confederacy and the Woman's Relief Corps.

In the days before annual national conventions, this "great mass meeting of 8,000 R.C. Friends" was staged in San Francisco on April 18, 1916, the highlight being a telephone call from Boardman in Washington to Marshall Hale, chairman of the meeting. The first national convention was held October 4–8, 1921, in Columbus, Ohio. Although the turnout was "very disappointing," according to one speaker, it wasn't for lack of trying. Guests included President Warren Harding, Field Marshal Lord Allenby of Britain, Marine General John Lejeune, and others. To entice its members, the Southern Division chartered trains at reduced rates to bring delegates to Columbus.

"The American Red Cross is the only volunteer society now authorized by this government to render aid to its land and naval forces in war," said U.S. President William Howard Taft on August 22, 1911. "Any other society desiring to render similar assistance can do so only through the American National Red Cross." The proclamation, based on the organization's congressional charter, reinforced the public view of the Red Cross as a semigovernmental agency and paved the way for broad support of its work with the military in coming years.

The American army occupies Vera Cruz, Mexico, in April 1914, to protect U.S. citizens there. With this move, the Red Cross decided finally to set up a definite plan of foreign relief after three years of sporadic help along the border. The Executive Committee called the public's attention to the organization's charter from Congress and began systematically helping American troops as well as the starving refugees. American Red Cross involvement in Mexico would not end until 1917. (National Archives)

"Civilians in Saltillo, State of Coahuila, Mexico, are in many cases eating donkey flesh and cactus . . . many are dying."

Red Cross News Release 1915

53

By the time Brigadier General John Pershing (center) led his expeditionary force into Mexico in March 1916 to protect U.S. interests, the Red Cross had limited its involvement with the refugee problems there, considering them a Pan-American concern. But the call-up of the National Guard in June got the Red Cross busy on the home front, collecting money and supplies for the families of the men being sent to the Mexican border until the government could make funds available.

An advertisement for Boardman's recollections, **Under the Red Cross Flag,** published in 1915. In the preface, she notes: "No effort has been made to produce a detailed and complete history of the organization here or elsewhere. Such would require years of study and scores of volumes, for which there was neither time nor ability, and for which the general public has no desire."

3. Expansion and Decline

The year 1917 finds the country answering the call to war in Europe. President Woodrow Wilson turns to the American Red Cross for help and urges the people to support the organization in its important role of assisting the military. Patriotism is alive everywhere. Red Cross workers march together into the conflict, with the confidence of the nation behind them.

The war emergency brought great change almost overnight. President Wilson announced the formation of a War Council to run the Red Cross and turn it into an efficient "arm of the government." A Junior Red Cross emerged to rally the nation's youth behind the war effort. Millions of volunteers began sacrificing their free time to help overburdened staff as old services expanded and new ones appeared—motor corps, canteen, production, and others. The nursing service, already seasoned in overseas relief, took on new importance, providing a constant stream of women for service with the military despite obvious danger.

Internally, the power base shifted. Eliot Wadsworth, a strong vice-chairman, controlled the Central Committee, overshadowing Mabel Boardman. And the all-male War Council, whose legality she questioned, chose to sidestep her, making decisions on its own. Boardman, relegated to a secondary role, resigned herself to bringing about the formation of a Woman's Advisory Committee and generally overseeing volunteer work. She would never regain her former authority.

In the early weeks of the war, the War Council, headed by Henry P. Davison, concentrated on raising money to finance the Red Cross mission overseas. It took advantage of the patriotic mood sweeping the nation to launch a $100-million war drive, which filled the days with zany events, bazaars, block dances, "Kick the Kaiser" parties, etc. Americans responded generously, quickly turning the organization into a multimillion-dollar corporation. The Red Cross treasury swelled from $200,000 at the outset of the war to $400 million in less than two years. But with success came a few complaints—allegations of dishonesty and immorality rumors, which haunted the Red Cross for decades.

America's new patriotism also affected the role of the Red Cross overseas, bringing it face to face with the concept of neutrality. In 1914, when war first exploded across Europe, the Boardman administration chartered a "mercy ship," filled it with doctors and nurses, and sent it off on a highly popular crusade to help the wounded of every belligerent nation, allegiance aside. From then on, Red Cross personnel demonstrated the Red Cross ideal of neutrality through their work with refugees and the wounded. With America's entry into the war, the Red Cross responded to the national mood. It stopped crossing the lines to assist, but announced that no one seeking its help would be turned away.

The war turned the organization into a powerful social force. Volunteers and staff at home served the active military and the returning disabled. Institutes for the blind and the crippled were opened and valuable contributions were made in veterans hospitals. Overseas, work spread from field hospitals to meeting the rehabilitation needs of nations whose social structure had been destroyed.

By the time the armistice was signed in the French railway car at Compiègne in 1918, Red Cross personnel were scattered from the British Isles to Siberia's far reaches. The troops would begin returning home while the Red Cross remained on, engaged in massive relief programs for refugees and victims of the Bolshevik revolution in Russia. At the same time, a worldwide pandemic of influenza, which killed more Americans than the fighting, forced the Red Cross to prove again that it was as ready for service in peace as it was in war.

By 1919, the world could look forward to a League of Nations that was established to bring a lasting peace. Red Cross societies made a peace move of their own. On the suggestion of Henry P. Davison, chairman of the American Red Cross War Council, the various societies formed a League of Red Cross Societies, whose aim was to provide mutual aid in times of great national need. It would be a lasting monument to Red Cross idealism.

War had set the stage for explosive growth within the American Red Cross. But the real test lay ahead in an America that had grown weary of war, with its casualty lists and its often meaningless heroics. Volunteers and contributions tapered off rapidly. The Red Cross would desperately seek ways of revitalizing the nation's interest in it while trying to withdraw gracefully from costly overseas programs for which there seemed to be little support and no visible end. It would prove to be a difficult task.

There will be little of sleeping to-night;
There will be wailing and weeping to-night;
Death's red sickle is reaping to-night
        War! War! War!

"The Call"
from *Rhymes of a Red Cross Man*
Robert W. Service, 1916

The lull before the storm. Shortly after this picture was taken on June 28, 1914, at Sarajevo, Bosnia, Archduke Franz Ferdinand of Austria (in hussar's hat and standing in front of the center car) and his wife were assassinated The incident motivated the start of World War I. A Red Cross official, Ernest J. Swift, obtained the photograph, which reportedly had been suppressed, from a Serbian photographer in 1919. According to his report, "After the ceremony, depicted in the photograph, the imperial auto turned about and proceeded down the avenue extending along the river. Turning into a side street by mistake, the chauffeur stopped his car to back out. At this moment, a boy of Serbian blood, but a Bosnian subject of Austria, stepped to the curb, leveled a revolver and fired at the Archduke. The first shot missed and the Archduke's wife threw herself across his body to protect him. The Serbian shot again and killed both."

The war in Europe allowed the Red Cross to display its impartial humanitarianism. Within weeks of the outbreak of war in Europe in 1914, a Red Cross mercy ship sailed across the Atlantic loaded with doctors, nurses and medical supplies for assistance to all nationalities.

The "mercy ship" slips out of New York harbor on September 12, 1914, bound for Europe with its Red Cross nurses and doctors, an event accompanied by a cacophony of boat whistles, cheers, brass bands and the singing of "The Star-Spangled Banner." The Red Cross kept the chartered ship only six weeks because public interest and financial support for the crusade waned, but the work in Europe continued with the wounded and refugees on a limited basis until America entered the conflict in 1917.

Assistant Secretary of the Navy Franklin D. Roosevelt suggests that Boardman replace the German crew aboard the S.S. Red Cross, leased from a Hamburg shipping line, which she did. However, some of the German crewmen stowed away, as did others. One Milwaukee father wrote Boardman, urging her to be on the lookout for his adventurous son, who could be recognized by the "tatoo of a snake on his left forearm." And one nurse writing to Jane Delano reported that at least two stowaways had been detected and looked as though they were "making their home on the coal boxes." Eleven others were put ashore before the ship left New York.

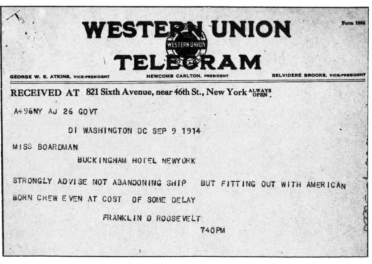

Letters home during the long voyage to England. "The Lusitania *sent a wireless at 8 P.M.," wrote one nurse, "saying we were coming to a storm and to prepare for it, everything is being tied fast and tacked down. Prayers and a hymn. Sister Helen posted the beautiful Prayer that Lord Roberts gave to every soldier who went to the Boer War for the Nurses to copy."*

A Red Cross doctor from Washington, D.C., atop the American Hospital in Munich with two convalescing German patients in 1915. A Chicago Herald newspaperman reported that he found a "splendid American Red Cross corps" in Germany and that "intense gratitude is felt for the hospital work of the American Red Cross. Exactly the same feeling is manifested in England and France." The organization was active in other areas as well. The American Red Cross Sanitary Commission joined forces with the Rockefeller Foundation to battle the ravages of typhus in Serbia, losing medical personnel in the process. Doctors and nurses also served in Russia, the Balkans, Austria and Hungary.

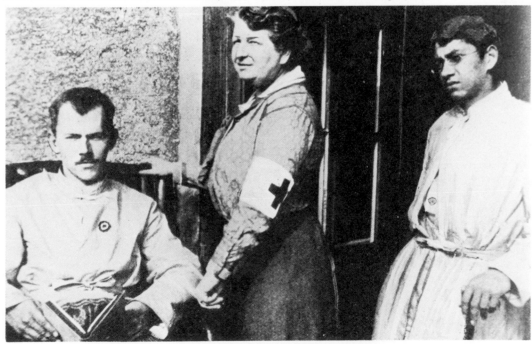

Its relief funds exhausted, the Red Cross withdrew nearly all its medical personnel from Europe in 1916, despite its successful work with the wounded and epidemic victims. America's entry into the war in 1917 against the Central Powers brought them back in force.

A German bombardment of Le Panne, Belgium, in 1916 sends American Red Cross nurses scurrying toward their sandbagged bunker with orphans in their charge. (National Archives)

President Wilson quickly mobilized the American Red Cross behind the U.S. war effort and appointed a carefully selected War Council to run it.

The War Fund drive in June 1917 netted over $100 million, surpassing its goal and encouraging the War Council. "It is hard to get a democracy in action," said council member Charles Norton, "but America is waking up. We in the Red Cross, Mr. Davison, the War Council, fortunately are free from red tape, and if we have the money, we can act with speed. Without money we can do little or nothing."

Men who know how to make money kick off the first War Fund drive in June 1917. Here John D. Rockefeller, Jr., parades for the Red Cross in New York City. Such activities helped the Red Cross net $400 million during the war.

Opposite:
The President of the United States and the War Council. "I have today created within the Red Cross a War Council to which will be entrusted the duty of responding to the extraordinary demands which the present war will make upon the services of the Red Cross both in the field and in civilian relief," said President Woodrow Wilson on May 10, 1917. The council assumed most of the executive committee's duties but its main task, in Wilson's words, was "to raise great sums of money for the support of the work to be done and done upon a great scale." Standing in the front row (from left to right): Robert W. DeForest, Red Cross vice-president; Wilson; William H. Taft, central committee chairman; and Eliot Wadsworth, vice-chairman. Rear row (from left to right): Henry P. Davison, War Council chairman, and fellow members Grayson M. P. Murphy, Charles D. Norton and Edward N. Hurley.

The Jewish community gave generously during the war. These Red Cross chapter workers are busy on New York's Lower East Side. As early as 1916, President Wilson issued a Red Cross proclamation calling for a Contribution Day for the Aid of Stricken Jewish People. The President said: "I feel confident that the people of the United States will be moved to aid the war-stricken people of a race which has given to the United States so many worthy citizens." At the time, some nine million Jews had been made refugees by World War I and were wandering aimlessly around Europe.

President Wilson felt personally committed to the organization's fund-raising success during World War I. He instructed Admiral Cary T. Grayson, later to become chairman of the Red Cross, to gather up sheep and put them to grazing on the White House lawn, which he did. "He appointed me shepherd of the flock," said Grayson. "When shearing time came I reported to him that we had a little over a hundred pounds of wool. He told me to send two pounds of this wool to each of the states, with instructions for the governors to have it auctioned for the benefit of the Red Cross . . . the total amount raised in this, my first Red Cross work, was $50,000."

Volunteers were plentiful during the war days. They came to the Red Cross for varied reasons, but mainly out of patriotism. One nurse wanted to become involved because "her family had always taken an active part in disturbances of the nation."

Counting on the nation's patriotism and humanitarianism to help it meet the military's need for nurses, the Red Cross set up recruiting stands on street corners. It enrolled 29,000 professional nurses, all but 9,000 of them eventually serving with the military. Outfitting them for duty overseas was expensive. In addition to stockings, tunics, capes, shoes and other accessories, they needed steamer rugs and life-preserver body suits for crossing the submarine-infested Atlantic. Also suggested, but not required, were warm underwear, a "cake of Johnson's foot soap" and corn plasters. (National Archives)

Opposite:
Sister volunteers in the San Francisco Motor Corps pose while helping to pick up scrap items for the war effort. The volunteers, who were sworn in as policewomen to give them added authority, supplemented government efforts to move troops and supplies at home and helped the organization conduct various relief activities as needed. The corps grew to 12,000 members in the summer of 1918, a high point. Motor service ambulances had covered more than 3.5 million miles by February 1919.

Members of the newly organized Junior Red Cross at Weatherford, Texas, in 1917. The idea of a Junior Red Cross grew out a proposal by Dr. Henry Noble McCracken, president of Vassar College. The idea was that they would raise funds, make useful items for "suffering children in foreign lands," and do all the things that the adult members had no time to do. "We will let them see democracy at work," said the War Council, "so that they may know what to do tomorrow." President Wilson made the movement official on September 15, 1917, telling American youth that they now could share in the "best work in the great cause of freedom." By February 1919, the Junior Red Cross had nearly twelve million members. (Weatherford, Texas, Democrat)

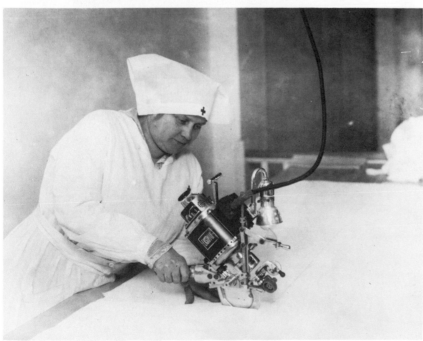

A production service volunteer cuts gauze at the Omaha, Nebraska, chapter in 1918. The material was used for making bandages for the troops.

Knit one . . . purl two. Members of the Cincinnati, Ohio, fire department learn how to knit socks, scarves and sweaters for the troops in their spare time under the guidance of Red Cross volunteers. Chapter volunteers knitted nearly eleven million articles of clothing for American troops and sailors during the war.

Mabel Boardman chats with a young soldier at a canteen station in New York, as he waits for the train that will take his unit to the port. A portable stove stands in the back-ground. (National Archives)

As Boardman struggled to set up the Woman's Advisory Committee, she received a letter from John M. Glenn, general director of the Russell Sage Foundation, which provided much support to the Red Cross. He believed in assigning women to social boards because they had something to offer, not because they were women, adding: "unsuitable women are more troublesome than men because they have to be treated with more consideration."

The Woman's Advisory Committee on the steps of the national headquarters in Washington. Boardman (in uniform at right) overcame the opposition of Vice-Chairman Eliot Wadsworth to establish the group in 1917. The committee's main function was to coordinate volunteer activities for American women seeking an outlet for their patriotism. She successfully argued that the men belonged at the front and in war industry while home front activities should be left to the women. Her feud with Wadsworth over her having an appropriate room in the newly completed headquarters and other matters led Chairman Taft to warn her not to hinder the work of the War Council. "This is not a question of women's right," he said. "This is a question of the best way to meet a great emergency . . . to secure the best results under the circumstances." Although she took Taft's advice, she told him, in reference to Wadsworth, "no one can run the Red Cross as a dictator." The situation mellowed considerably in later years.

Some of the first black nurses to serve with the U.S. Army stand outside their quarters at Camp Sherman in Chillicothe, Ohio. About 1,800 black nurses were certified by the American Red Cross for duty with the military. However, the Red Cross had no control over their assignments to hospitals, which meant that unless a "colored cantonment" had need for them, their services were often not utilized. The situation changed with the flu epidemic of 1918–19, when medical help was scarce. (Armed Forces Institute of Pathology)

The Red Cross encouraged all races to give service. "We can show you in the Red Cross," said Henry Davison, "as fine a collection of Baptists, Methodists, colored people and every other kind of people as there is on the face of the earth." However, the military units were segregated and the racial composition of volunteer services at the chapter level reflected the prevailing attitudes of the community.

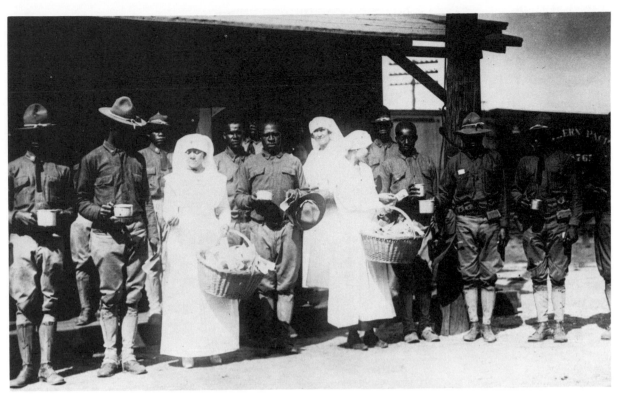

A segregated army unit shipping out is visited by Red Cross canteen workers.

"SINGER CLAIMS TO BE THE MODEL." An operatic mezzo-soprano, Marguerite Fontrese, from Cleveland, Ohio, reportedly turned down an offer from impresario Fortune Galle in order to sing at Red Cross rallies and pose for Foringer's *The Greatest Mother in the World.* Many persons claimed to have modeled for Foringer, and rumors even circulated that the artist and his model planned to go into vaudeville and the movies. Foringer said that the real model for this poster was "Miss Agnes Tait, an artist herself, and not a professional model." (See color insert, Plate 12.)

69

Fund posters reflected idealism, but campaign methods employed a lighter touch.

Harry Gardner, the "human fly," scales the tall Temple Bar Building in New York City as the featured Red Cross performer in the Second War Fund drive in May 1918. (National Archives)

Americans find an outlet for their pent-up frustration with the war through Red Cross fund-raising events. This boy kicks "the Kaiser" outside New York City Hall in May 1918.

GENERAL PERSHING Cables:

"No other organization since the world began has ever done such great constructive work with the efficiency, dispatch and understanding, often under adverse circumstances, than has been done in France by American Red Cross in the last six months."

The appeal of the Great War was a fund raiser's dream. The American Red Cross was able to raise in a week enough money to dwarf the treasuries of some nations. "He was asked for a donation which would have supplied a prince's ransom," wrote one Indianapolis fund raiser. "As I watched that man's face during the interview, saw interest awakened, then pity, and generosity, caught sight of the struggle between his desire to respond fittingly to the appeal which had touched him, I felt as if I were looking on while a man found his soul."

General Pershing lauds the Red Cross in 1918, one of the many times he helped promote its activities.

Red Cross fund raisers sweep up money in New York with a vacuum cleaner as servicemen exhort the crowd to give more during the second big fund drive in May 1918. They reportedly emptied the vacuum cleaner bag many times. (National Archives)

The war in Europe called for a massive undertaking by the American Red Cross. In France alone, it operated out of 551 locations, providing canteen, medical and general health and welfare services for the American Expeditionary Forces. Personnel wearing the Red Cross insignia were scattered from the British Isles and western Europe across the Middle East to the far reaches of Siberia.

A band plays while canteen workers refresh troops on their way to the front in France. The **Red Cross Bulletin** *described the need for the service in a 1918 article: "Traveling from America to France is no pleasant job. It involves a trip to the American port from the training camp, a long and tedious voyage across the Atlantic on a crowded boat, a day or two in a rest camp and finally, a long trip to the front. A soldier who has arrived in France after this journey needs every comfort that can be given to him on his way to the front." Standard fare was coffee, hot chocolate and sandwiches.*

American and French servicemen enjoy themselves at an American Red Cross canteen in Bordeaux, France. It was one of many run by the organization for Americans and their allies. There were also seventy-five railway canteens in France that served hot meals and sometimes offered dormitory space to troops rolling toward the front. All told, they served about fifteen million troops.

"The Flying Squadron." The men who drove for the Red Cross overseas had a certain dash and flair about them. This unit in Britain was organized like a fire department to deal with coastal sinkings. The men slept on the premises and could respond to calls for supply trucks within three minutes. (National Archives)

The Outpost Service in the Argonne forest in 1918. Red Cross workers stayed close to the lines, advancing with the troops. Their usual equipment was a stove or rolling kitchen, thermos containers for hot chocolate, tobacco, toothbrushes, shoestrings, writing paper, and sometimes even hard chocolates and crackers. One unit served hot coffee to troops fighting in the mountains of northern Italy at an elevation of 11,000 feet. A 1918 press cablegram from Paris reported: "Red Cross men have not stopped their work in the St. Mihiel battle since the Americans opened the attack. They have followed steadily behind the advancing troops." Workers served 160,000 gallons of hot cocoa in that one battle alone.

Scottish villagers receive Red Cross clothing and supplies for survivors of the troopship Otranto, *which sank off the island of Islay, Scotland. The organization ran a system of warehouses in the British Isles to aid American survivors of shipwrecks. The Red Cross, keeping enough materials on hand to outfit six thousand persons, started the program in 1918, following the sinking of the troop transports* Tuscania *and* Moldavia.

"I'm willing to confess it takes nerve of more than one variety to handle unconscious boys and legless men all day long. But it was worth the day's work to hear a legless man whisper, 'Ah, the Red Cross! Vive les Américains!' "

Red Cross Ambulance Driver
France, 1918

Ambulances in France. Forty-seven ambulance companies were recruited by the American Red Cross for duty overseas. The organization brought together 4,760 men, trained them in first aid, and then turned them over to the army. All saw service overseas, and many were decorated for bravery. At least 127 of them lost their lives. In Italy, the American Red Cross directly operated five ambulance sections. The men handled more than 148,000 cases, logging nearly 635,000 miles in doing so.

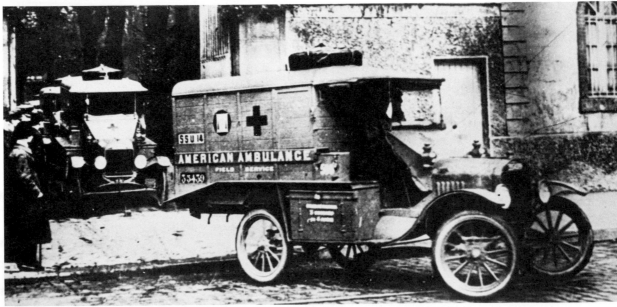

Red Cross dogs located the wounded and led stretcher bearers to them. The dogs were trained to bring back the wounded man's helmet or other item of clothing as a way of alerting the medical units. This dog served on the battlefields of France. (National Archives)

"The wounds from the trench mortar didn't hurt a bit, and the machine gun bullet just felt like a smack on the leg by an icy snowball," reported Lieutenant Ernest M. Hemingway (on crutches) after being wounded along the Piave River in July 1918. "I got up and got my wounded to the dug out." Before collapsing, the Red Cross ambulance driver who would one day win the Nobel Prize for Literature carried an Italian comrade to safety, thereby earning Italy's second highest award, the Silver Medal for Valor. The eighteen-year-old Hemingway was one of several ambulance drivers who distinguished themselves as writers in the postwar years. Others include John Dos Passos, Robert Hillyer, Malcolm Cowley, William Seabrook and Louis Bromfield. (Hemingway Collection, Kennedy Library)

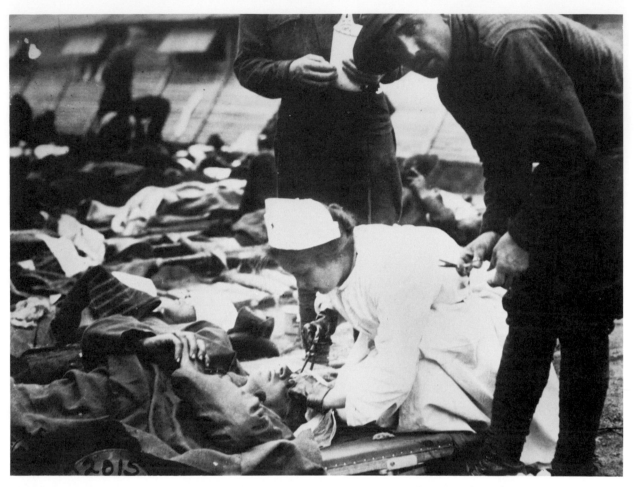

A Red Cross nurse at the 326th Field Hospital in France bathes the eyes of gassed patients from the U.S. Army's 82nd and 69th Divisions.

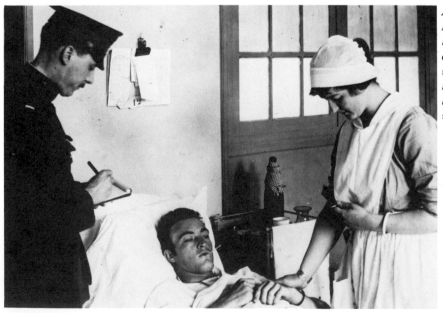

A wounded soldier is attended by Red Cross personnel in one of the twenty-four base hospitals that the organization ran jointly in France with the army. The hospitals treated nearly 92,000 wounded, losing less than 1,500 to their wounds. (National Archives)

Jane Delano exchanges views with one of her nurses during an inspection trip to an army training camp at home. While in France, she fell ill with ear problems, underwent several operations at a base hospital in Saveney, France, and died April 15, 1919, at age fifty-seven. "Poor old Miss Delano," wrote nurse Elizabeth Ashe in Intimate Letters from France 1917–19, *"has had a mastoid operation and I fear there is little hope for her. She has been ill ever since her arrival." Delano, posthumously awarded the Red Cross Distinguished Service Medal in gold, was interred temporarily at Saveney, where groups of German prisoners reportedly saluted as her casket was carried by. "She devoted herself in the most unselfish manner to a great work," said President Wilson, "and gave her life for it." (Harris & Ewing)*

Now the birds are singin', singin', and I'm
home in Donegal,
And it's Springtime, and I'm thinkin' that I
only dreamed it all;
I dream about that evil wood, all crowded
with its dead,
Where I knelt beside me brother when the
battle-dawn was red.

"The Convalescent"
from *Rhymes of a Red Cross Man*
Robert W. Service, 1916

77

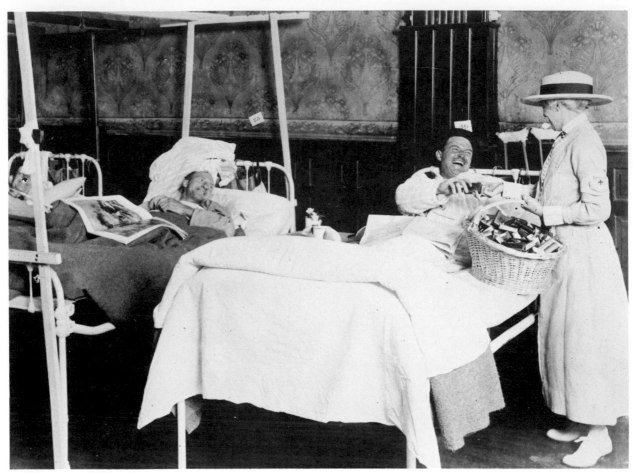

Books, comfort items, and a friendly volunteer help keep morale up in a base hospital in France. (Library of Congress)

One hospital worker received a letter from a patient, saying: "You sure have got some service. Received the razor, soap, toothpaste and brush O.K. The Red Cross is the goods all right. When you came through the ward and said to us fellows you'd have those things there next day that old croaker in Bed 9 piped up: 'Don't get excited boys: it will be like some of the other promises we hear.' I liked to died of joy when we got those five packages from the Red Cross just as you said we would and now that old grouch, he'd like one too. You sure treat us great. I'm going to tell the home folks to give all their money to the Red Cross."

A rest porch at an army hospital in France, where the wounded can enjoy the sunshine.

A convalescing soldier in France receives word at a canteen hut that all is well at home. The Red Cross Home Service helped the men stay in contact with their families and assisted them with personal problems. Although the service relied on letters, rapid communications were sometimes needed to relay messages to the United States. Cables were used in "particularly distressing cases, to the number of 250 a day" from the Paris headquarters of the Red Cross when large numbers of U.S. troops were being sent into action late in 1918. After hostilities ended, the Red Cross found it had to continue its overall service until mid 1919 because of the large number of inquiries from worried families. (National Archives)

U.S. prisoners in German-held territory at Metz, France, celebrated Thanksgiving with parcels from the American Red Cross in 1918. The Bureau of Prisoners' Relief, located at Bern, Switzerland, had looked after about 3,700 American prisoners by the time the war ended. In addition to food, clothing, and comfort items, the Red Cross workers also delivered mail from home. Ninety percent of the parcels sent to the American prisoners reached their destination. The bureau also had a Division of Allied Prisoners, through which Italian and French prisoners could be helped in special cases.

The **Northern Pacific** *unloads its wounded off the coast of Long Island in 1918, as a fire burns furiously on its stern. A Red Cross doctor and nurse wait on the beach to assist. (National Archives)*

Opposite:

A searcher for the Home Communication Service in France talks to a group of soldiers about some of their comrades who are missing in action. Searchers gathered news and other information about wounded and sick men, or details about deaths and soldiers missing in action. The information was relayed to distraught relatives, who often received only a brief government notification. The Home Communication Service also photographed the graves of American soldiers buried in France and sent the photographs to the families. More than 170,000 such photographs were taken. (National Archives)

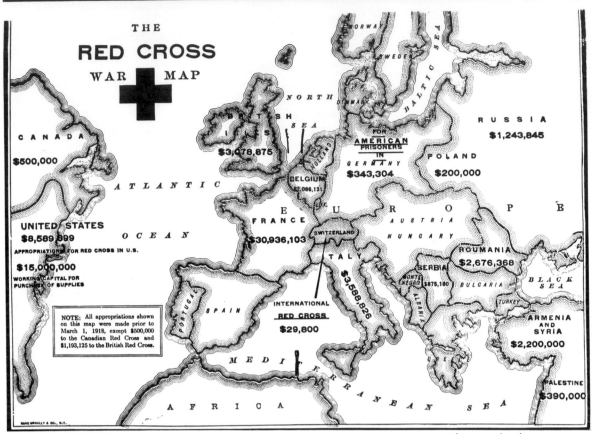

A map of Red Cross expenditures at home and abroad in early 1918. By February 1919, the organization had spent $273 million on war work.

Deadly influenza began sweeping the country in September 1918, prompting the surgeon general of the United States Public Health Service to call on the Red Cross. About fifteen thousand nurses, dieticians, and others were recruited and sent to work in military camps, hospitals, coal fields, munitions plants and shipyards, where they remained until the epidemic finally subsided, in the spring of 1919.

The Spanish influenza pandemic killed some thirty million people worldwide from 1918 to 1919 and took a heavy toll of life in the United States. More than 540,000 of the millions who fell ill in America died. Medical personnel were in short supply and there were reports that some funeral directors were so busy that they often were unable to pick up bodies on the same day they were called. The Red Cross met the emergency by making its nurses and volunteers available and by setting up tent cities to ease the overload on hospitals.

Production volunteers at the Butte, Montana, chapter wear the influenza masks that they are producing for the troops overseas. Similar operations around the country produced clothing and surgical dressings to the tune of over 371 million relief articles in the twenty months ending February 28, 1919. The Junior Red Cross contributed 10 percent of that total. Originally, the volunteers' uniforms were to have had a red cross on the bodice. In her book The Fabric of Memory, *Eleanor Robson Belmont, a volunteer on the Woman's Advisory Committee, which set uniform standards, noted that the first instructions read: "The red cross on workers' uniforms should be in proportion to the bust measurement." That, she recalled, "gave our male leaders a setback."*

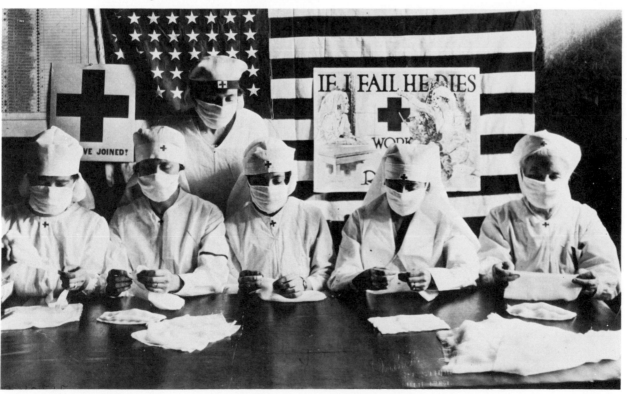

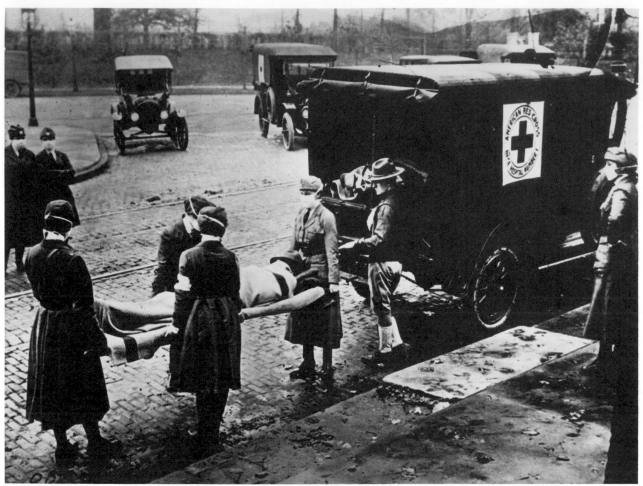

Motor Corps volunteers in St. Louis, Missouri, pick up victims of the influenza epidemic in October 1918 in response to appeals to the Red Cross from the United States Public Health Service, which had labeled the outbreak a "national calamity." By the time the epidemic had run its course in the spring of 1919, the Red Cross had recruited some 15,000 nurses, nurses' aides, and other volunteers to care for the ill. A total of 223 nurses and 5 dieticians are known to have died giving service to the military and civilian population at home.

Red Cross workers were not spared during the epidemics. "I am happy because I've tried to be a real American," said nurse Elizabeth McWilliams of Somerville, New Jersey, who died in October 1918, before her troop ship reached Britain. She had been working with influenza victims aboard ship for two days prior to her death.

The armistice brought peace to the trenches on the
western front in November 1918. When the troops
went home, the Red Cross stayed on to care for civilian
victims and the soldiers left behind in Russia to protect
Allied interests.

*Newly released prisoners of war celebrate signing of the
armistice by taking a ride on buses run by the American Red
Cross for servicemen visiting London.*

"Now that the hope of victory soothes her pains, France remembers that since the very beginning of her trials, her boys fighting on the front or wounded in the field, her widows and orphans, and all those who needed help and could be reached, have received the heartiest support, both material and moral, from the American Red Cross. When peace has come, when wounds are cured, when ruins are repaired, when orphans have grown [to] men, France shall never forget."

Raymond Poincaré
President of France
November 1, 1918

Field Marshal Pétain expresses his gratitude for the work of the American Red Cross with the French soldiers through an autographed photograph.

86

1. This calendar appeared shortly after the Spanish-American War.

2. Cover for the American Red Cross Bulletin. *The magazine provided a vehicle for the organization to tell its story while obtaining funds through membership subscriptions and advertisements.*

3 and 4. *The mystique of a Red Cross Nurse. Margery Kay of Detroit, Michigan, who served in Paris, typified the glamorous image the nurses projected. Although the Red Cross tried to discourage the attitude, they were viewed romantically throughout the war, as in the popular song "The Rose of No Man's Land." (National Archives)*

5. A Norman Rockwell cover which could be interpreted in a number of ways. It appears the young woman is more interested in her stack of love letters than in the war tales her ardent suitor tells her.

6. A Red Cross Magazine *dedicated to the Junior Red Cross carries a cover by Norman Rockwell.*

7. *Veterans of the Civil War, proudly wearing their* **Grand Army of the Republic** *uniforms and Red Cross pins, flank a doughboy in this magazine cover by Norman Rockwell in June 1918.*

8.

9.

10. Patriotism ran high following U.S. entry into World War I. People found an outlet for it through the Red Cross, especially at fund drive time. The poster at the right carried impact because it commemorated the first American soldiers to give their lives in World War I.

11. *Most popular of the many posters painted during World War I was A. E. Foringer's* The Greatest Mother in the World, *a work originally done for the Second War Fund campaign, May 20–25, 1918.*

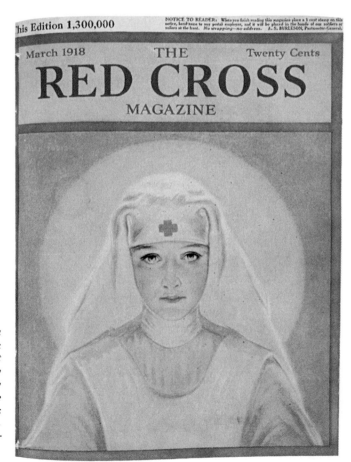

12. *Artists frequently put Red Cross women on a pedestal, as this issue of the* Red Cross Magazine *illustrates. The magazine was read both at home and at the front. It contained works by such authors as Edna Ferber and Henry Morgenthau and others, and paintings by the likes of N. C. Wyeth, who created items specifically for the magazine. By placing a one-cent postage stamp on the magazine, the reader at home could send it overseas.*

13. *A Harrison Fisher Roll Call poster for 1918 that became popular. The original poster was autographed by Fisher for Al Jolson, the jazz singer.*

14. *1918 Christmas Roll Call, by Jessie Wilcox Smith.*

15. A 1921 fund-raising poster calls on Americans to support the work of the Red Cross with disabled former servicemen.

16. The Junior Red Cross celebrates its tenth anniversary in 1928.

17. Poster reflects the many activities of the Junior Red Cross.

18.

IS YOUR CHAPTER PREPARED ?

AMERICAN RED CROSS DISASTER RELIEF SERVICE

19. The reputation of the Red Cross rode on the performance of its chapters during times of disaster. This poster was an admonishment to those who were unprepared.

20.

21. N. C. Wyeth's 1933 *Roll Call* is among the finest of all American poster art.

22. *The appeal for money in 1940 to help embattled Britain, France and all the Eastern European countries facing Nazi Germany's armies.*

YOUR RED CROSS NEEDS YOU!

23. A James Montgomery Flagg poster painted for the December 1941–March 1942 War Relief Fund drive, is used to recruit volunteers. The national director of volunteer service, Pauline S. Davis, offered the following excerpted credo to America's women in the bleak days of January 1942:

> *America is in a war which encircles the earth. America is fighting a world revolution which would destroy us.*
> *The old adage that "Men Must Work and Women Must Weep" no longer holds good; in the hard months ahead if some American women weep they will be working too....*

SUPPORT THE RED CROSS
NATIONAL CIO WAR RELIEF COMMITTEE

24.

FIGHTING MEN NEED NURSES

Sign Up at the Red Cross Recruiting Station

25.

Your RED CROSS
is at his side

1944

WAR FUND

1944 WAR FUND

26.

27. *The last of the "Greatest Mother" posters. Painted by Lawrence Wilbur for the 1943 war fund drive, it was one of many done by the artist for the Red Cross over the years.*

28. *The 1941 Roll Call poster by R. C. Kauffman. The appeal for money to finance Red Cross operations abroad was launched on December 8, the day the United States and Britain declared war on Japan.*

29.

30.

31. *America responded to appeals for blood by voluntarily donating on a free basis some 13.5 million pints between February 1941 and September 1945, when the program ended. At the peak of the program, January through June 1944, the Red Cross was operating 35 fixed blood centers and 63 mobile units. Donations averaged nearly 111,000 pints weekly or one pint of blood every two seconds.*

32.

33.

34. The fortieth anniversary of the Junior Red Cross.

35. The last poster for the Red Cross by Norman Rockwell. The 1951 painting depicted workers from three major services moving into action— a doctor with a bottle of whole blood, a trained first-aider with a kit, and a uniformed volunteer who represented the backbone of the American Red Cross.

An American veteran of the Polish army receives a snack on the docks in New York following his return in 1920. Some 2,300 other Poles left the U.S. during World War I to help Poland fight the Germans.

All eyes turned toward peace in 1919. The League of Nations was established, and with the blessing of world leaders, a League of Red Cross Societies was created in the same year. As directed by Article XXV of the League of Nations Covenant, the world's Red Cross Societies began "the improvement of health, prevention of disease, and mitigation of suffering throughout the World."

Henry P. Davison visits London in September 1918 on his way to France for an inspection tour of American Red Cross facilities. Although Davison's work with the War Council ended in 1919, his legacy lives on through the League of Red Cross Societies, to which the American Red Cross belongs. He proposed that the national societies form an association that could turn war readiness toward the problems of peace. Davison died May 13, 1923, following brain surgery.

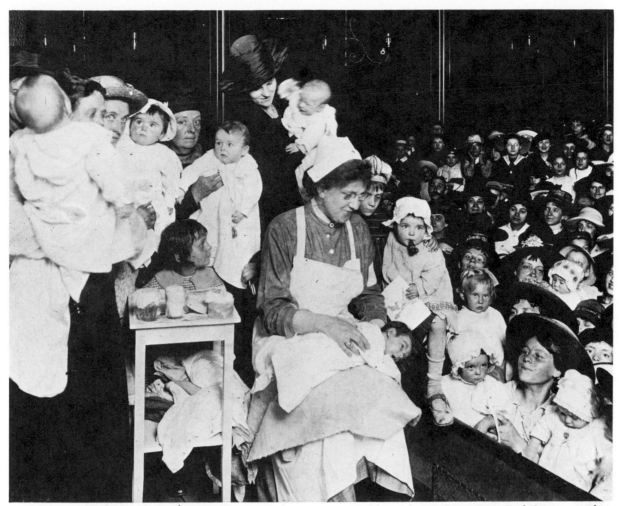

Mothers at Saint-Étienne, France, in the postwar period learn from an American Red Cross nurse how to care for their babies. The Red Cross sent doctors and nurses to several nations following the armistice to help local medical personnel set up clinics and health courses. (National Archives)

Opposite:
French refugees flock to an American Red Cross facility for food, shelter and medical care. The Red Cross operated about twenty-five civilian hospitals and convalescent homes for war refugees, plus numerous health centers, clinics and mobile dispensaries around France. More than 1.7 million French were assisted with their basic needs and, after the signing of the armistice, with their resettlement. (Library of Congress)

Red Cross relief activities for the millions of refugees in Europe went on until the early 1920s. The Red Cross also engaged in other worldwide relief, sending personnel and over one million dollars to China to counter the starvation that swept the country's northern provinces in 1920–21.

Typhus scourges the eastern front. The "Great White Train" of the American Red Cross covered more than four thousand miles in Siberia, administering to the needs of Russian troops and civilians. It carried Red Cross doctors, nurses and attendants and was responsible for saving thousands of lives that might have been lost to the disease. A British doctor observing the Red Cross handle typhus victims in Serbia in 1915 reported that the disease was "far worse than typhoid fever and even worse than the Black Death." It was spread through unsanitary conditions.

Long after the war with Germany had ended, civil war flared in Russia as the Bolsheviks fought the loyalists for power, particularly in Siberia. Troops from several countries, including the United States, guarded the Trans-Siberian Railway line to keep it from being damaged by marauders, while an American Red Cross medical car traveled the railroad providing assistance to the sick and wounded, such as this Czech soldier. Red Cross personnel remained in Siberia, feeding and medically treating refugees, until the spring of 1920, when the Red Army overran the loyalists.

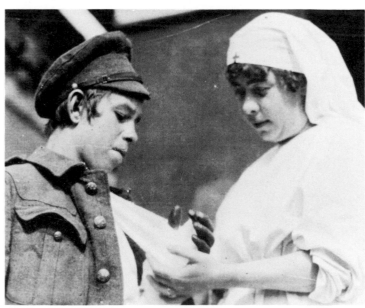

A 1920 newspaper article about Annie Laurie Williams, a Red Cross nurse with the medical relief section of the Siberian Commission, who put a Russian bully in his place.

American Woman Tackles Russian Bully in Omsk

Red Cross Worker Rains Blows on Him in Rough-and-Tumble Fight

OMSK, July 17 (via Vladivostok, August 10), (correspondence of the Associated Press).—A certain Russian bully learned something about American women that will lurk in his memory for some time through an encounter a few days ago with Miss Annie Laurie Williams in the freight yards at Omsk. Miss Williams' name will be familiar to many as a welfare worker. She is now with the American Red Cross and was one of those twelve women chosen to remain behind when the others were hustled out of Omsk by the American Ambassador to Japan, Roland S. Morris, to escape a possible Bolshevik invasion.

The Russian was attempting to climb aboard a car in a refuge train in which were several girls. The girls were trying to shut the car door against him when Miss Williams appeared and grappled with the intruder. She landed two blows on his jaw and then they rolled together down the embankment. As they arose she gave him another.

Two Czech soldiers then came to her aid and, but for Miss Williams' intercession, would have finished the bully, who was allowed to retreat and ponder on the strange ways of American women.

Two Russian youngsters wearing Red Cross pins wait for the click of the shutter aboard a chartered Japanese ship taking them from Vladivostok, Siberia, to Petrograd, Russia, in 1920, a roundabout trip that would take four months. They were among 782 Russian children being returned to their parents by the American Red Cross following two years of separation. The children had been sent away because of wartime food shortages. When their return by rail was made impractical because of revolutionary war flaring across Siberia, the Red Cross chartered the Yomei Maru *in July of that year to take them home via the Panama Canal, San Francisco and New York. The voyage was filled with personal hardships despite the presence of Red Cross personnel.*

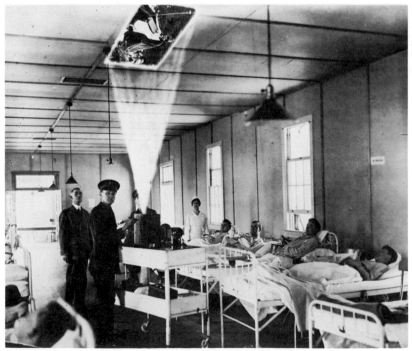

Red Cross workers at an army hospital in 1919 show convalescing patients motion pictures on the ceiling, using a machine designed by Red Cross Captain R. Hayes Hamilton. The films were sometimes beneficial. At a Red Cross hospital in France, a young soldier suffering from shell shock reportedly laughed himself to recovery while watching Charlie Chaplin. Since that time, the report went on, "he has been able to talk and laugh as of old." Recreation activities at hospitals were handled by the Red Cross, while the YMCA and other organizations provided them for the able bodied. (Library of Congress)

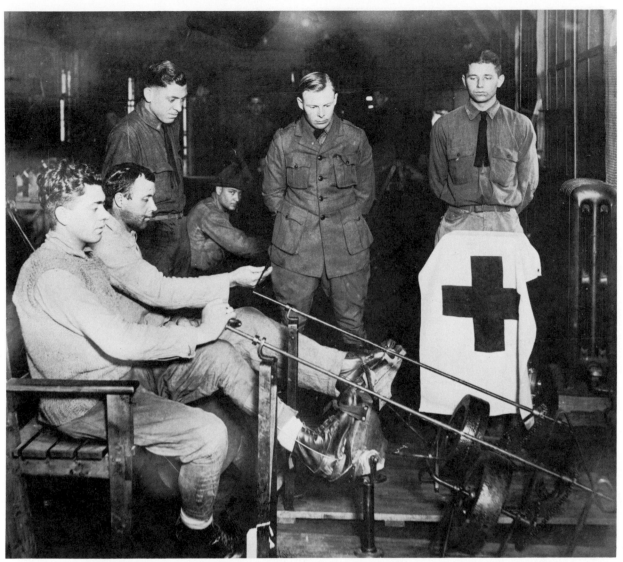

A Red Cross rehabilitation program at an army hospital in 1919 provided therapeutic exercise for disabled veterans. The patients used a "circumductor" designed to loosen up stiff ankles and knees. The Red Cross also ran the Institute for the Blind in a Baltimore suburb, an involvement that started May 25, 1919. At "Evergreen Estate," veterans were taught new vocational skills and braille and were given recreational opportunities. Eventually, responsibility for disabled veterans was passed on to the U.S. Veterans Bureau. Occupational therapy and recreation activities, both pioneered by the Red Cross, continue to be a mainstay of veterans hospitals. (Library of Congress)

With war activities ended, Red Cross chapters rushed to fill the void by helping returning veterans readjust to civilian life, particularly the maimed and disabled, who were the most likely candidates for the Lost Generation.

Hollowing out a wooden limb. As a result of a private grant, the Red Cross opened an Institute for Crippled and Disabled Men in New York City in 1917. Artificial limb making was an important part of the instruction program at the institute. As the volume of disabled veterans needing help increased in the postwar period, the Red Cross found the task too great and gave it up in late 1919, letting the government take responsibility for their rehabilitation. (Library of Congress)

A newspaper cartoon reflects a new image of the Red Cross by the time the war effort ground down in 1921. It was a far cry from the idealistic "Greatest Mother" themes of 1918.

4. Evolution

The postwar era challenges the Red Cross anew. Its leaders stand at a crossroads, wondering what the organization's role should be, while millions of volunteers vanish into the vast vacuum of the "roaring twenties." A strong new leader and a spate of economic and natural calamities eventually set the organization on its modern-day course.

Two years of postwar activity found the Red Cross trying to maintain its bigness while putting together programs that would serve the American people best and keep them interested in the organization. It had an obligation to the military and the refugees overseas, but those activities were quickly sapping the financial reserves needed to assist the vast army of veterans. Public support was at a low ebb. Red Cross chairman Livingston Farrand focused the organization's efforts on public health nursing and family welfare work, which drew criticism from social agencies that felt they were being displaced. Chapters helplessly watched their volunteers leave and complained that the national headquarters expected too much from them and the country. Membership dropped off dramatically along with the funds it normally brought. The problems of peace were proving to be too much and Red Cross leaders were stymied. Reorganization again seemed in order.

A quiet Virginian would lead the organization out of the morass and provide it with solid leadership until 1935. Judge John Barton Payne, who had served as secretary of the interior under President Wilson, succeeded Farrand, who resigned in 1921. Payne moved quickly to pare down the fat and still growing Red Cross services, espousing the philosophy that the organization could be strong without war, and without reliance on emergency work to justify its existence. He startled fellow volunteer leaders by stressing the need for the Red Cross to meet social demands not being met by other agencies while fulfilling its charter obligations of disaster relief and service to the military and veterans. And he envisioned staff and volunteers working closely together to bring this about.

Nature would trouble the world relentlessly between 1923 and 1937, and out of misfortune, the American Red Cross would regain its former prominence. The Mississippi Valley floods of 1927 prepared the Red Cross for even more devastating flooding in the mid thirties. And the widespread drought of 1930–31 saw the Red Cross provide extensive relief while turning down congressional moneys that would have compromised its reliance on voluntary contributions and workers. The volunteer ranks swelled, then came down again as President Roosevelt attacked the country's depression with New Deal legislation that improved public service enough to diminish the need for voluntary help. But there was no substitute for Red Cross expertise. In 1933, the Red Cross began distributing federal relief supplies to the army of the unemployed, an acceptable compromise for a proud organization resisting government control.

By 1939, retention of volunteers was the least of Red Cross problems. The world, which was to have been "made safe for democracy" through World War I, echoed with the sounds of Nazi jackboots and the *Banzai* cries of invading Japanese armies. The Red Cross embarked on a massive relief program to aid refugees. Ships riding deep in the water hauled medical supplies, food and clothing to the victims, the emblazoned red cross on their sides providing minimal protection from submarine attacks. At home, Americans watched the war clouds gather and cheered the Red Cross efforts. They volunteered their time to help with traditional programs and a newly burgeoning one, blood collection services, which would soon become a lifeline for the nation's fighting men and women. After two decades of evolving into an efficient peacetime organization, the Red Cross was again standing on the threshold of world war.

The new chairman of the Red Cross, Dr. Livingston Farrand, on a visit to Seattle, Washington, in October 1919. He supported Davison and Wadsworth in their move to "get new blood into the Executive Committee," according to outgoing Chairman William H. Taft. In a letter to Vice-President Robert DeForest, Taft said Farrand was being pressured into seeking the removal of Mabel Boardman from the Executive Committee. He recommended that Farrand "retain Mabel Boardman on the Executive Committee," even though Wadsworth and Davison "were against it," pointing out that "Mabel Boardman had founded the Red Cross and had created the organization out of which the War Council grew; that it was her efforts that built the building which he [Farrand] would occupy as the head of the Red Cross; that no matter whether Wadsworth and Davison differed from Mabel, he ought not to regard their advice." But Boardman lost her bid for reelection to the Executive Committee in the 1919 balloting, as well as her position as national secretary. By 1920, she was again national secretary and by 1921, back on the Executive Committee.

General Haller of Poland decorates the Red Cross flag in October 1923 with his country's highest medal in commemoration of the American society's relief efforts in the postwar period. Mabel Boardman (left) clasps the flag. In cooperation with the Polish American Children's Relief Commission, the Red Cross operated a chain of health centers throughout Poland, turning the project over to the Poles in 1922. A similar award was presented in 1923 by Austria as testimony to the American Red Cross work with the destitute there.

Commodore Longfellow and members of the YWCA Life Saving Corps tour places where free swimming lessons are being given in 1920 during the Red Cross Learn-to-Swim Week. This famous Red Crosser posed in a New Year's card as King Neptune of the deep. Longfellow died on March 18, 1947, just three months after his retirement. To the end his slogan had remained: "Every American a swimmer, every swimmer a lifesaver!"

Red Cross instructors at a boy scout camp in Kentucky around 1925 pair off learners about to enter the water for the day's lesson. The caps served an important function, because they identified the learner's level of ability. "Sink easies" wore red caps; beginners, green; swimmers, blue; and lifesavers, white. The boy scouts gave the Red Cross an ideal opportunity to promote water safety. In addition to working closely with the scouts at summer camps, Longfellow wrote material that was included in the popular Handbook for Boys, *which was second only to the Bible in copies sold in 1934.*

Johnny Weissmuller (left), Olympic champion swimmer who held seventy-five world records, poses with Joseph Law, director of the Red Cross Life Saving Service for the Southwestern Division, in 1923 at Lake Geneva, Wisconsin. Weissmuller, who climbed to fame as Tarzan in the movies in the 1930s and 1940s, often worked as a volunteer at Red Cross aquatic schools.

Members of the Red Cross Women's Life Saving Corps pose on a beach at Jacksonville, Florida, in 1923. The corps had six thousand members at the time. The Red Cross Courier *reported that women were good at swimming because "they possess natural buoyancy and power of coordination which makes the art preeminently their own." Although they had their own corps, women took the same lifesaving tests as the men.*

Fire roared through Tokyo and neighboring Yokohama, Japan, thirty minutes after an earthquake struck on the morning of September 1, 1923. Some 200,000 persons died, and another two million or so were left homeless, as the two cities were almost completely destroyed. A typhoon lashed the area later in the month, blowing down most of the temporary shelters.

Japan's earthquake victims received extensive help through and from the American Red Cross in 1923. Critics of U.S. policy charged during World War II that had Japanese officials been reminded of the disaster assistance, World War II might have been averted.

Distribution of relief supplies from the American Red Cross to the victims in Tokyo. The organization launched an American Red Cross Japanese Relief Fund, which eventually helped two million victims. Red Cross chapters raised some $12 million for the operation, nearly double the original goal. The funds provided food, clothing, medical goods, lumber and building supplies, a memorial hospital, and a large grant to the Earthquake Relief Bureau.

This cartoon appeared in the 1923 Asahi newspaper in Tokyo. Its caption declared: "America has lived up to its reputation in the Japanese calamity of being the most sympathetic nation in the world."

An American Red Cross truck carrying supplies bogs down in China.

"Mounted on a crude sedan chair," said Ernest Bicknell, chairman of the Red Cross commission investigating famine in China, "I was borne proudly upon the shoulders of four nimble-footed bearers. In all, we had 14 donkeys and 14 men in our outfit. Our wanderings took us 125 to 150 miles into the interior." There, Bicknell reported finding the "lowest depth of poverty."

Flooding became an ongoing problem for the Red Cross
in the twenties and thirties.

*The Great Mississippi Flood in the spring of 1927. The Cincinnati–Hamilton County Chapter in Ohio
calls on Americans to help the Red Cross raise the millions needed to help the flood sufferers. The chapters
eventually raised more than $17 million. The Red Cross set up 154 refugee camps, caring for more than
325,000 persons in a reconstruction program that lasted for more than one year. Millions of dollars were
spent on clothing, food, seed for planting, furniture and vocational training. Since over 53 percent of
the victims were black, a Colored Advisory Commission was set up under Dr. Robert R. Moton, president
of Tuskegee Institute, an effort that proved to be a model of interracial cooperation. More than five
million acres of farmland had been ruined during the flooding, but it brought an unexpected benefit
to the area—the introduction of high-grade cotton, seed and livestock by the Red Cross.*

Relief workers bring food to stranded families who are waiting for the waters to subside at Wheeling, West Virginia.

THE BEACON LIGHT.

When the *Arkansas* Gazette *ran this editorial cartoon on May 5, 1927, more than 25,000 persons were severely affected by the flooding that had been going on for more than six months due to continually heavy rains in the central states. By April, the disaster had turned into a national calamity as levees crumbled along the Mississippi. The Red Cross provided heavy assistance in the early stages as well as the late. By May 1928, the organization had finally finished its reconstruction program, which included replenishment of seeds and other agricultural items and immunization against rampant smallpox, malaria, typhoid fever and pellagra.*

Junior Red Cross members in 1928 in Newark, New Jersey prepare gift cartons for shipment to needy children overseas.

A poster used by a company in 1926. Industry's need for first-aid training for employees grew enormously in the early twenties, when machinery generally lacked protective devices. To meet its own needs, the Bell Telephone Company allowed laymen to teach first aid to employees in 1923, which proved successful. The Red Cross followed suit in 1925, dropping the requirement that instructors be physicians.

American Presidents continued their support as honorary chairmen of the Red Cross.

"Silent Cal" greets Red Cross Gray Ladies and disabled veterans of World War I in the White House garden. First Lady Grace Coolidge stands to the far left. Noted for his brevity in speeches, President Coolidge was outdone by Mabel Boardman on one official occasion, when her introductory speech consisted of no more than "Ladies and gentlemen, the President."

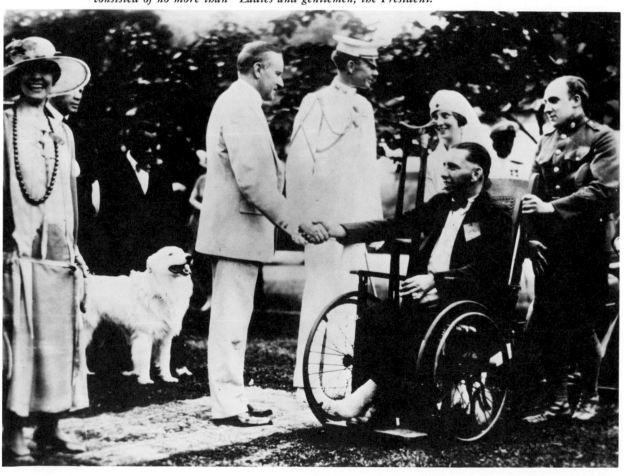

Humorist Will Rogers practices with his lariat in 1926. A strong supporter of the American Red Cross during World War I, he was made an honorary life member of the Central Committee in 1927. In June of that year, he said, "We are so used to the things the Red Cross does that we sometimes just forget to praise them. Lord, what a blessing an organization like that is. I would have rather originated the Red Cross than to have written the Constitution of the United States." In that same year, he proudly reported to Chairman Payne that he had booked twelve benefits for the Red Cross. In 1933, the organization established the Will Rogers Fund after he contributed $25,000 for support to Red Cross services "in danger of lapsing through lack of funds."

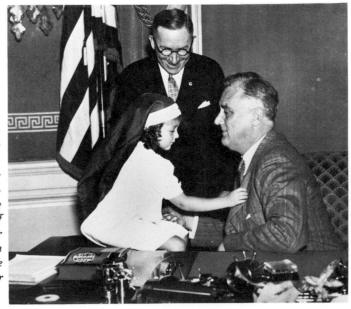

Five-year-old Phyllis Smith enrolls President Franklin D. Roosevelt as a Red Cross member in 1934. Acting Red Cross Chairman James Fieser watches during ceremonies in the Oval Office. By that time, the Red Cross was already deeply involved in the President's efforts to relieve the unemployment problem through a massive infusion of money and agricultural products. FDR saw the Red Cross as a means of getting Americans off the "dole," and said in 1933, "when any man or woman goes on a dole, something happens to them mentally, and the quicker they are taken off the dole the better it is for them during the rest of their lives."

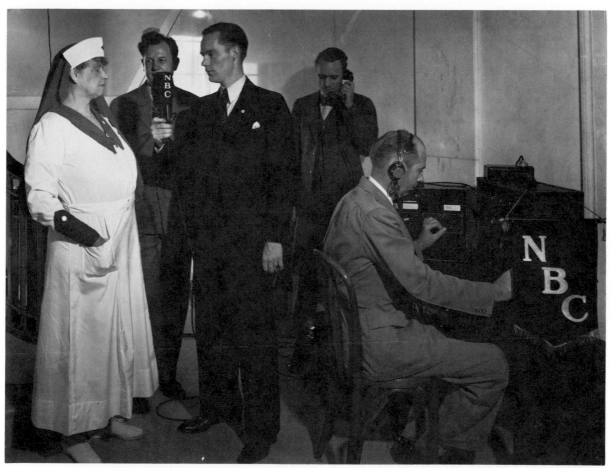

Mabel Boardman gives an on-the-spot interview in 1934 at the District of Columbia Chapter, where she was chairman of Volunteer Services in addition to her national duties. Boardman describes the activities of the chapter for WMAL announcer Red Kimball. Although she was a native Ohioan, she knew Washington intimately. In September 1920, President Wilson had named her the first woman commissioner of the District of Columbia, and in that capacity, she had inspected every hospital and welfare agency in the city during the next several months. A Washington Post *article in 1939, entitled "A Portrait of a Victorian," said of Boardman: "Her eyes are gray, with a glint of blue in them. In repose her face resembles Queen Mary's, but the smile that illuminates it is wholly lacking in frosty majesty." In the early 1920s, the Prince of Wales had a similar impression upon meeting her at national headquarters. As he walked into her office, he reportedly said, "Good Lord—there's Mother!"*

"The Red Cross knows no barriers of race or creed," said Chairman Payne in the thirties. "The American Red Cross has no political opinions and only one religion—Service to humanity."

Mabel Boardman knew exactly what roles she thought men and women should play in the Red Cross. Rejecting suggestions that she should be the top executive in the organization, she once said, "The chairman must always be a man. The public has more confidence in men executives."

Voluntary service with the Red Cross was at a low ebb
in the mid thirties, reminiscent of 1925, when Chairman
Payne estimated that only about half of the some 3,500
local chapters were "carrying on some form of volunteer service." Boardman, director of national Volunteer
Services, complained in 1937 that too many chapters
thought of the program as merely "a way to sell the Red
Cross," making her feel like a failure.

*Remembering the role of the American Red Cross in Japan's natural disasters
over the years, citizens of Nikko turn out to welcome Chairman Payne, who was
attending the Fifteenth International Red Cross Conference in Tokyo in the
fall of 1934. Alarmed by the apparent militancy of Japan and Germany, he
appointed a committee to study the organization's preparedness for war service
in that year, calling it the Military Relief Committee. It helped prepare the Red
Cross for the rapid expansion of services required by World War II. Payne died
January 24, 1935, two days before his eightieth birthday, following an appen-
dectomy complicated by pneumonia.*

"The Red Cross needs no war," was Judge Payne's philosophy. He saw the Red Cross as having a mission in
the social field as well as during war and disasters. He
also believed volunteers should be guided by profes-
sionals at the operational level, ideas that Boardman
and her supporters resisted. Payne stressed the need for

volunteers and professional staff to work together to form a "definite forceful organization" that could deal with both America's calamities and her social needs. He told Boardman in 1922 that she should either accept the concept or "the present organization should be scrapped, and you should go back to the time when you sat at a desk alone and had a membership of a few thousand." He added: "The whole must march along as a single army, not the volunteer in one direction and the permanent workers in another."

Red Cross policy regarding unemployment and strikes came into question frequently between 1928 and 1932. This ad ran in a Des Moines, Iowa, newspaper in 1928, and attacked the organization's policy of "abstaining from national relief in unemployment distress." Local chapters were allowed to give assistance, but they often lacked the resources to be of real help. In 1932, socialist Norman Thomas, executive director of the League for Industrial Democracy, charged in his speeches that the Red Cross had refused to give relief to strikers. Chairman Payne countered that Thomas was mistaken, that during the winter of 1931, "we fed something like three million unemployed, including the striking coal miners of Kentucky and other localities."

Attention
MINERS AND ALL LABORERS

Do you remember when the Miners in the Mystic coal fields were on strike in 1927 and 1928?

Do you remember when the Miners were on strike or "locked out" in the Appanoose fields in 1928?

Do you remember the stories of human suffering in the mine fields during that terrible winter?

Do you remember the heroic efforts of the "Bandana Gang," composed of men and women in the Miners Union and Auxiliary, to allay the suffering of those impoverished Miners and their families?

Do you remember that the first appeal to the Red Cross for aid to these suffering people was made in 1927?

Do you remember that a second appeal for help was made to the Red Cross in 1928?

Do you remember that HUBERT UTTERBACK of Des Moines, Democratic candidate for Congress in the Sixth District, was Chairman of the RED CROSS for the State of Iowa at that time?

Do you remember that he refused to give the slightest aid through his organization to these destitute miners and their families?

Is this the kind of a man laboring people would have represent them in Congress? Labor cannot support a man for public office who has turned his back on them in their darkest hour of trial and suffering!

Remember this "record" when you go to the polls on Nov. 6.   —31

Dust storms, grasshoppers and drought plagued American farmers in the western and midwestern states, adding to the woes borne by a country bogged down in Depression. A sympathetic Red Cross assisted, but staunchly refused government aid for fear of compromising its principles.

The Courier-Journal *in Louisville, Kentucky, decries moves by Congress to appropriate $25 million to the Red Cross in 1931 to deal with drought relief and general relief to the unemployed. Chairman Payne and the Central Committee voted to turn down federal aid because drought relief was already being provided by the Red Cross and could be completed without government funds, and relief for the unemployed was being taken care of by other public agencies.*

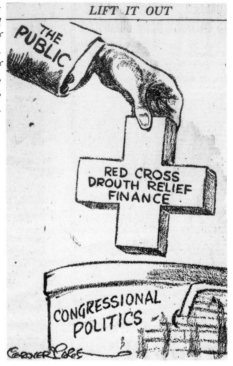

A Red Cross volunteer at Lonoke, Arkansas, dispenses foodstuffs to drought victims in 1931, part of some five hundred boxcar loads donated to the organization. Chapters distributed to the victims more than $11 million worth of food, clothing and seeds for planting. Regional manager A. L. Schafer reported that many drought victims were "still in their homes, widely scattered and inaccessible. Dulled and hopeless with misfortune, livestock gone, every resource exhausted, initiative killed, they sit and wait. Help must reach them or starvation will." In order to survive, many sold all their possessions, including their clothes, for a few cents, dug roots in the woods to eat, and slept under leaves on the floor.

The nation's newspapers hailed the American Red Cross in 1931 as a bulwark against socialism and a monument to self-help when it turned down a $25 million congressional appropriation to help drought victims and the unemployed. It preferred to rely on its own ability to solicit contributions from the public. "The Red Cross has," said Chairman Payne, "after the most careful consideration, determined that the welfare of the Red Cross and those it is now helping, and will help in the future, requires that it continue its historic, voluntary role, and refuse to be drawn into politics." Public pressure and a deteriorating economy forced the Red Cross to reverse its stand in 1932.

An overjoyed farmer in Arkansas smiles his thanks after receiving from the Red Cross a box of seeds for planting, a mainstay in the organization's drive to make the drought sufferers self-sufficient again. Despite their plight, many of the victims were reluctant to seek aid even, as one relief worker cabled, "when visitors find obvious starvation and other wants. Some cry when asked as to their plight." The Red Cross fed over half a million families during the drought of 1930–31.

A chapter Gray Lady sits behind the wheel of the car that will give a convalescing soldier at Walter Reed Army Hospital an outing. Another Red Cross worker holds the door open. President Roosevelt's New Deal legislation took away many of the traditional volunteer jobs by putting unemployed people on the federal payrolls to perform them. As voluntarism lost its urgency, the recruitment of chapter volunteers suffered. In addition, many had the idea that the Red Cross wanted only "the best class of people." Mabel Boardman did little to help when she said in 1934, "Women of wealth and position have frequently told me they've never been so happy in their lives as when doing Red Cross work," a notion that held little appeal during the Depression. This "ladies bountiful" image long continued to vex the Red Cross leadership.

New Deal legislation during the Depression diminished the need for voluntary service in the community, but provided an unexpected dividend for the Red Cross. After years of decline, a new interest in first aid was evident as the result of federal work programs being initiated to lessen unemployment.

The Gray Lady uniform had a lot to do with the popularity of the service, a factor Mabel Boardman capitalized on by introducing to the other volunteer activities service pins and chevrons for hours served. The use of uniforms became widespread in 1938 after two hundred uniformed volunteers had paraded at the national convention of Red Cross chapters, bringing the cheering crowd to its feet.

A 1935 Gray Lady reads for a hospitalized youngster. The uniformed Gray Lady Service had wide appeal for volunteers, as did the Braille Transcription Service. The work was meaningful, the training authentic, and the activity filled the void left when the Red Cross pulled its professional staff out of the Veterans Administration hospitals in 1930. By 1931, the service was expanded as more needs developed.

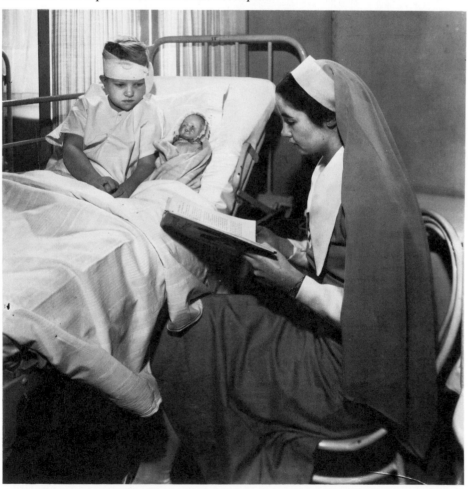

Unemployed men line up for government food items made available through the services of the 3,700 Red Cross chapters. Succumbing to public sentiment, the Red Cross assisted the government in what many Red Cross leaders negatively viewed as "charity work," for which the organization was not designed. Relief during true disasters, they thought, was the real mission of the Red Cross. The good that the work accomplished could not be denied—85 million bushels of wheat and 80 million bags of flour distributed to nearly 6 million families, and other services. The Red Cross also set up distribution of more than 844,063 bales of government cotton.

Young men working with the government's Civilian Conservation Corps help pack Red Cross food into trucks for hauling to refugee camps in the Cincinnati, Ohio, area. Through such cooperation with the government, the Red Cross was able to wrap up its operations by August 1937. In little over six months, the organization clothed, housed, fed and gave medical care to over half a million people. The operation required the services of some 10,000 staff and nearly 45,000 volunteers.

The Civil Works Administration tried to protect unskilled workers being put on the government payroll by requesting that the Red Cross train them in first-aid techniques, which it did. A safety program was set up, and the Red Cross was asked in 1934 to provide training through its chapters. The Red Cross trained and certified more than 48,000 workers.

A Red Cross first-aid instructor demonstrates how to put an arm with a suspected break into a sling, part of a federal safety program in 1934.

Lewis Hine rose to fame as a social photographer. He was hired by the Red Cross in 1931 to capture the human side of America's latest calamity. (See photo above and on page 113.) The supervisor who hired him reported to his St. Louis office that Hine apparently "knows his business, but like all photographers he seems to need a lot of personal guidance."

The Red Cross began setting up Highway Emergency First Aid Stations in 1935 at gas stations and other places near the major roads. By 1939, there were nearly 5,000 posts and mobile units manned by people trained in Red Cross first aid. Highway deaths had multiplied dramatically during the twenties and thirties. In 1934 alone, 34,000 Americans died on the roads and one million were injured.

Red Cross feeding station at Compton, California. An earthquake rocked the Los Angeles vicinity March 10, 1933, killing 95 persons and injuring 1,332. More than 31,000 homes were destroyed or damaged, requiring the establishment of Red Cross "concentration camps" to house the many homeless. Veterans organizations, church groups and local welfare agencies gave the Red Cross outstanding assistance in the operation, which President Roosevelt urged the nation to support.

Stefan Vasilakos hands over a paper bag full of money to a volunteer from the District of Columbia Chapter in 1936 in support of that year's Roll Call. The peanut vendor received special permission from Eleanor Roosevelt to operate outside the White House gates during the campaign.

The Community Chest, forerunner of United Way federated fund raising, was active during the twenties and thirties, but very few Red Cross chapters participated in it for fear of losing control over their financial destiny. Unable to resolve differences with the Community Chest, the delegates to the 1929 national convention recommended that chapters stay out of federated fund raising. There would be little chapter participation before the early 1950s.

Coastguardsmen and Red Cross volunteers await refugees fleeing rising waters at Yazoo, Mississippi. Unlike later flooding, the rise of water was gradual in February 1933, allowing the Red Cross to evacuate families and livestock. The absence of swift currents also prevented heavy property damage. The organization assisted nearly twelve thousand families with food and distributed some thirteen thousand packets of seed to help with the spring planting.

Shirley Temple appeals for public support on behalf of the American Red Cross in advance of the 1936 Roll Call.

Floods along the Ohio and Mississippi rivers bring the federal government and the American Red Cross together at a refugee camp in 1935 near Forrest City, Arkansas. Harry Hopkins (center), President Roosevelt's appointee to the Flood Emergency Committee, chats with a family made homeless by the disaster as Red Cross vice-chairman James L. Fieser (far right) listens in. Hopkins, close adviser to Roosevelt, was no stranger to the Red Cross, having served with its Gulf Division during World War I in Home Service, and later as manager of both the Gulf and Southern divisions. He resigned in 1922 after deciding that the job kept him away from his family too much.

No optical illusion. A Red Cross damage surveyor inspects houses tipped over along River Road in Louisville, Kentucky, during the Ohio and Mississippi floods in the spring of 1937.

Natural disasters combined with economic ones gave America a bad spring in 1936. Flooding dominated the Midwest and Northeast, and tornadoes traced a deadly path across the Southeast, stretching Red Cross disaster funds to their limit.

Opposite:
Floodwaters crest at Saltsburg, Pennsylvania, on March 19, 1936. Heavy snowfalls followed by intense rain and warm temperatures triggered unprecedented flooding of urban areas in the eastern states from New England to Pennsylvania. In April, tornadoes complicated matters, enlarging the affected area to twenty states. The American public responded to Red Cross appeals by contributing nearly $8 million, the best showing since the war days. More than 102,000 families had received Red Cross assistance by June 30 of that year.

Cooks prepare a side of beef for the pots that will feed thousands taking refuge in a disaster camp at Forrest City, Arkansas. The food was prepared under the supervision of Red Cross dieticians and sanitary inspectors.

Governor Martin Davey of Ohio referred to Red Cross relief workers such as these·as "unsung heroes." An official 1937 report on the Ohio-Mississippi flooding said: "Volunteer women prepared and served food until they were nerve-wracked; boatmen navigated the swift currents in towns and across the flooded fields to save the lives, personal belongings, and livestock of the victims. There were many stories of personal bravery and sacrifice."

Tornadoes ripped through the South in the spring of 1936, devastating areas of Mississippi, Georgia and North Carolina, leaving over three hundred dead and thousands injured. Victims sought shelter in various Red Cross facilities, including a boxcar camp at Tupelo, Mississippi, referred to by newspapers as Boxcar City. Each boxcar was furnished with a stove, electric lights, steps and cots. Community showers and sanitary facilities were also provided, as were visits by a Red Cross public health nurse. Said one reporter, "I'll swap my room at the hotel for one of these layouts anytime!"

Stunned disbelief. Red Cross workers and others gather in the business section of Gainesville, Georgia, following the tornado.

The Providence City Hall awash at the height of the hurricane that lashed Rhode Island on September 21, 1938. The storm killed 494 people in its sweep through southern New England and New York. The Red Cross set up its disaster headquarters in Providence and disbursed aid to some twenty thousand homeless families before winding up the operation.

Public health nursing eased the pain of daily living for many affected by the downturn in the economy.

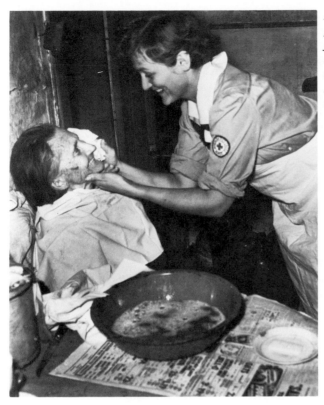

An elderly patient reflects the mood created by a visiting public health nurse in the hills of Pennsylvania, where funds for medical care were scarce. "In many rural communities," noted chairman Payne in 1925, "Red Cross is the only welfare agency." The organization's aim—make American families "self-supporting" through "constructive relief."

A Red Cross public health nurse boards the army transport St. Mihiel *at San Francisco in 1935, carrying a baby belonging to one of the families that the government is sending to Alaska to start an American colony. Some six hundred settlers from drought-stricken areas of the Midwest were given twelve-acre tracts in the wilderness of Matanuska, Alaska. The Red Cross nurses served under a contract with the government, providing necessary medical care for the settlers who were trying for a new life. "Our dads pioneered on the land in the Middle West," said one man. "They succeeded. So can we!"*

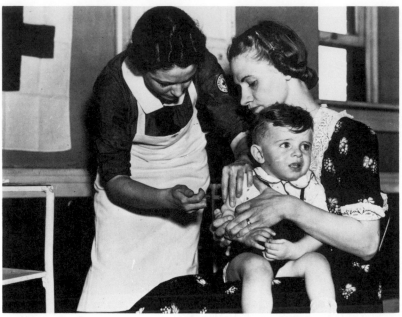

Regular baby clinics such as this one in West Virginia became a familiar sight in the 1930s, both in the cities and in rural areas, as Red Cross public health nurses pushed the fight against childhood diseases. The heyday of public health nursing was from 1919 until 1922, when the nurses mainly operated out of schools.

Walt Disney, famous film animator, stands next to the ambulance he drove briefly for the American Red Cross in postwar France, displaying his budding talent on its canvas in this 1919 photograph. Disney joined up at age sixteen.

Singer Connie Boswell, comedian Bob Hope, Charlie McCarthy and ventriloquist Edgar Bergen starred in the annual membership campaign on Armistice Day in 1939, while war was afoot in Europe. Highlighting the hour-long program was President Roosevelt, who said from the White House: "We of this fortunate country are already doing much in the name of humanity on behalf of the unfortunate victims of this unhappy war, and when the time comes for the Red Cross to ask your special help to continue this work, I am confident of your sympathetic response."

December, 1937   *The Red Cross Courier*

Everybody's friend, Walt Disney, brings his world-famous family into the Red Cross—with the help of Mickey

The possibility of war drew closer in 1939. Germany
had annexed Austria and invaded Poland.

*H. Sherbourne House, American Red Cross representative at Geneva, ladles
out soup during an inspection of Nazi-run facilities at Radom, Poland, in May
1940. He was trying to estimate the needs of refugees living there.*

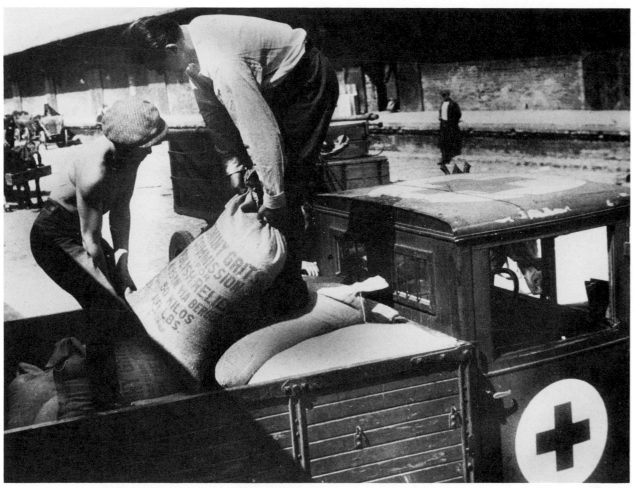

Hominy grits are unloaded at a Polish warehouse in August 1940, as part of the massive relief effort the American Red Cross had launched.

As its British allies engaged Hitler's force, isolationist America made a halfhearted attempt to ready itself for possible entry into the war. The Red Cross was already involved in a massive infusion of aid to the victims of war by 1940.

Using one of 435 vehicles donated by the American Red Cross, a worker for the Women's Voluntary Service, a British organization, hands out tea and sandwiches to rescue workers following a blitzing of London. The American Red Cross also sent ambulances to Finland in February 1940, after it was attacked by the Soviet Union.

"As President of the Women's Voluntary Services and on their behalf," said Queen Elizabeth of England on October 24, 1940, during London ceremonies marking the receipt of hundreds of U.S. vehicles, "I accept with gratitude this magnificent gift from the American Red Cross. I know these women and children who have been ruthlessly bombed out of their homes, and I am sure that they would wish to join with me in saying thank you from the bottom of our hearts."

The chapter's first shipment of surgical dressings made by volunteers is readied for the long journey to Britain in the fall of 1940.

A British nurse at a London hospital prepares for the night's casualties, laying out blood plasma and transfusion equipment. Since most of Britain's mobile transfusion equipment was left behind at Dunkirk following the British retreat in April and May 1940, the American Red Cross joined hands with the Blood Transfusion Betterment Association to launch a Plasma for Britain project, which operated out of New York's Presbyterian Hospital. The public response was immediate, and the first blood drawings took place on August 16, 1940. The Red Cross provided voluntary workers, donors and most of the money for the project, which ended January 17, 1941, after Britain announced it had enough plasma of its own. A total of 14,556 pints of blood had been donated for conversion into liquid plasma, but little had actually been used for fear that it had been contaminated during the voyage over.

Heavy losses by England early in the war, due mainly
to air raids, led to the launching of the Plasma for Britain project in 1940, a combined effort between the
American Red Cross and the Blood Transfusion Betterment Association.

*A mobile unit at Presbyterian Hospital in New York City in the winter of 1941. Dr. Drew (left) guided
the pilot project in its initial stages, as the Red Cross began providing dried plasma for the use of the
U.S. military. The dried plasma could be stored for relatively long periods of time, unlike the earlier
liquid form that was sent to Britain. The outgrowth of this Red Cross project was the nationwide
Program for the Procurement of Dried Plasma for the Armed Forces. Dr. G. Canby Robinson of Johns
Hopkins University became the first national director of the Blood Donor Service in July 1941.*

Plasma for Britain was an eye-opener for the government, which requested that the American Red Cross
and the National Research Council combine forces
again and provide dried plasma for the U.S. military.
On February 4, 1941, Red Cross volunteers went to
work at the hospital center, reporting to Dr. Charles R.
Drew, a physician who had supervised the Britain project and who had emerged as a leading authority on
mass transfusion and processing methods. A new agree-

ment in the fall of 1941 gave the Red Cross a continuing "charter" to enroll donors, draw their blood and ship it to processing centers. Before the first Japanese bombs fell on American ships, nine Red Cross centers were operating in the East and Midwest.

A New York Chapter mobile unit prepares for blood collections in the fall of 1941. The first visit by a mobile unit took place on March 10, 1941, when a trailer borrowed from the defunct Plasma for Britain program was sent to the Farmingdale, Long Island, chapter. But chapters were not new to blood collecting. The Augusta, Georgia, chapter started the first donor enrollment program in August 1937. By June 1938, eleven chapters, from the Northeast to the Southeast, were involved, and several others in the South were preparing to embark on similar programs. At the army's request, the Southeastern Pennsylvania Chapter in Philadelphia started collecting blood in September 1940 for research centering on the manufacture of dried plasma "in the event of war involving the United States."

An Air Corps plane arrives at Camp Hoffman, North Carolina, with dried plasma for use by troops on maneuvers shortly before World War II.

French boy scouts greet the **Cold Harbor** *upon its arrival in Marseilles in April 1941 with foodstuffs for the conquered French. The ship, delayed in Italy for security reasons, was the first mercy ship allowed through the British blockade after the fall of France.*

Letters from French mothers credited the American Red Cross with saving the lives of their children through the donation of milk. More than 2.5 million children benefited at French nursery schools, such as this one in Marseilles in June 1941.

President Roosevelt endorsed the unique status of the Red Cross, especially where fund raising was concerned, and supported the decision of the Central Committee to conduct fund campaigns as needed. The Red Cross, he said in a June 6, 1941, letter to the chairman, "must continue to be the agent of the popular will and the reliance of the government. It must have mobility and freedom of action. It must retain its name and emblem, as required by law and international treaty, for its own purposes."

War drives the tourists away from tiny Monaco in 1941, putting it into a depressed state. A relief worker pedals his way to a school where milk and children's clothing from the American Red Cross will be distributed.

Workers at Bayonne, New Jersey, fill a cargo hold with sacks of beans and flour destined for Greece in 1941.

A Chinese girl proudly wears a new dress made from American Red Cross wheat and rice sacks. After a few washings, the lettering runs and makes the garment a "pretty pink," according to the original caption of this 1941 picture.

Red Cross production work in the United States nearly rivaled that done during World War I. Chairman Norman Davis announced in November 1941 that chapter volunteers had made and shipped nearly 37 million garments and bandages for war victims in Europe and China.

Volunteers from the Manila Chapter of the American Red Cross gather in the residence of the U.S. high commissioner to produce garments for refugees in Europe in 1940.

The Japanese advance across China in 1941 sent refugees fleeing to the Philippines, where the American Red Cross helped the U.S. Army provide assistance.

A nurse with the Philippines branch of the American Red Cross consoles bewildered British children, two of 2,500 refugees fleeing China in the face of the advancing Japanese army in 1940.

Irving Berlin plays "Angels of Mercy" *for chairman Norman H. Davis, who announced on November 3, 1941, that the song, especially composed by Berlin to honor the Red Cross, would be the "official American Red Cross song." It was played publicly for the first time on November 11, launching the Roll Call drive.*

"The quickening pace of our defense program," said President Roosevelt in November 1941, "shows that our strength can be tempered to meet steel with steel, And voluntary enlistment in Red Cross work—through membership—will prove that we have the heart as well as the sinews to keep ourselves strong and free."

5. Rebirth

With the coming of the Second World War, Red Cross ranks swell to legion strength overnight. The "day of infamy," December 7, 1941, plunges the organization into immediate work at home while its machinery remains geared to helping refugees overseas.

Red Cross chapters opened their doors to thousands of new volunteers looking for a way to vent their frustration over Japan's surprise attack on Pearl Harbor. Enrollment in first-aid courses skyrocketed in a display of "invasion nerves." Blood Donor Service centers doubled and tripled their output, and the pace in production rooms across the country quickened as the making of surgical dressings took on new meaning. The first war fund drive was launched immediately, the $50 million goal seemingly too high. Within weeks chairman Norman Davis pushed it to $65 million in reaction to the magnitude of the mission. Red Cross officials watched in amazement as contributions pushed well beyond that goal in the first of many multimillion-dollar drives. The Red Cross was again America's sweetheart.

Riding on the crest of its renewed popularity, the Red Cross quickly expanded its services to the armed forces. It recruited nurses on behalf of the military, and provided social workers and canteen specialists to ease the discomfort of civilians being drafted. Within the Red Cross, efforts were under way to end segregation policies, which stubbornly prevented many blacks from obtaining positions at the professional level.

Shaking off the initial shock of war, America began unleashing its industrial might in support of hard-pressed allies in Europe and the Pacific. American women dried their tears and swept up their hair into bandannas, manning the factories and shipyards. Others joined the ranks of the Red Cross and similar groups sustaining the morale of the American people at home and in the foxholes. By the time the marines stormed up the beaches at Guadalcanal in 1942, more than three million volunteers were involved in Red Cross activities ranging from home nursing to civil defense. Young and old collected scrap, taught nutritional courses, and served in hospitals, where nurse shortages abounded. Their number more than doubled by 1944, and the jobs they performed were endless.

As the war progressed, prisoners became a problem to world governments. The American Red Cross cooperated with the U.S. government, taking on the task of shipping weekly food packages to some 115,000 American prisoners of war and more than 1.3 million allied POWs in Europe and the Far East. Volunteers worked on assembly lines at several centers in the East and Midwest, processing 1.4 million packages monthly. At the height of the activity, in 1945, twelve ships flying the Red Cross flag carried supplies from American shores for distribution through the International Committee of the Red Cross.

Years of war tested the nation and the Red Cross, but both grew stronger through the adversity. Despite occasional complaints about it, the organization became indispensable. The American public expected its Red Cross to be active in peacetime too, a leader in community involvement. When surveyed by a Gallup poll in 1946, Americans responded overwhelmingly in favor of the Red Cross keeping its greatly expanded services. Among those responding were many who had stared out from behind barbed wire, emaciated but alive because of Red Cross prisoner of war packages.

The postwar years provided a platform from which the Red Cross could display its newfound maturity. Pushing political ideology aside, it helped "tilt the horn of plenty" by spreading its amassed new wealth among war victims around the world. The American Red Cross would be able to boast that from 1939 to 1946 it had matched dollar for dollar the moneys given to it by the U.S. government for civilian relief overseas, and it was a fitting welcome for its new president in 1949, General George C. Marshall, architect of President Harry Truman's European Recovery Program.

As world crises cooled, so did the public's ardor. People still expected essential Red Cross services around the clock, but many felt that somebody other than themselves should provide the voluntary manpower. And there were new problems—minorities questioning long-standing policies, public requests for services of a non-emergent nature, costly disaster operations that strained dwindling Red Cross reserves, and others. But the climate was different. Within, the old leadership was gone, ended with the death of Mabel Boardman in 1946. Personal whims and racial prejudice were giving way to workable management practices. It was a changing world, and the American Red Cross would change with it in order to survive in the uncertain times of the cold war era.

The destroyer U.S.S. Shaw *explodes during the Japanese attack on Pearl Harbor, December 7, 1941. "We saw the planes diving, and there was a lot of shooting," said Walter Wesselius, a Red Cross executive on a field visit to the Hawaiian Islands. "The sky seemed so full of planes. Somebody behind me said proudly, 'These are swell maneuvers for a Sunday morning.' It wasn't until black smoke began to rise and blot out the whole harbor that a man nearby yelled, 'Maneuvers nothing. It's the real thing!' " Within minutes of the first attack, Red Cross volunteers, who had been practicing for possible air raids, went into action, providing first aid, shelter and transportation for military and civilians alike. When the planes left, less than two hours later, eighteen U.S. ships had been sunk, and the list of dead or missing stood at 3,219.*

Within minutes of the first attack on Pearl Harbor, Red Cross first-aid teams and nurses were on the scene, responding as they had been taught in repeated war drills.

Red Cross nurses and first-aiders give emergency care on park benches in Honolulu. All civilian defense on the island was organized under the Red Cross, and for months before the attack, volunteers had practiced operation "air raid precaution" and had ten emergency medical stations operational. The several thousand trained first-aiders proved invaluable in the wake of the attack, as the wounded sometimes waited for hours to be seen by a physician, often because they were cut off by flames. Sixty percent of the 960 seriously wounded suffered third-degree burns, according to one Red Cross report, requiring the heavy use of Red Cross plasma and sulfa drugs to pull them through.

The news that greeted Americans around the country the evening of December 8 signaled the coming of four years of new sacrifices. By the time this newspaper hit the stands, the American Red Cross headquarters had marshaled 1,000 trained personnel, supported by 1.7 million volunteers in the chapters, for service to the armed forces. It also launched a $50 million war relief fund drive. Some Red Cross leaders believed that the Japanese people would have turned away from war had American leaders allowed the organization's role in Japan's 1923 earthquake to be played up more in diplomatic circles.

The S.S. *Mactan,* chartered by the American Red Cross, sailed into the southern Pacific in January 1942, with nothing to protect it but the red crosses painted on its white bulkheads. It carried a Red Cross team of doctors and nurses and some two hundred seriously wounded soldiers from the beleaguered U.S. Army in the Philippines. The destination was Darwin, Australia, and the mission came at the request of General Douglas MacArthur, who believed the Japanese would respect the Red Cross flag. The ship reached port without incident while The Japanese navy monitored its progress.

Red Cross doctors and nurses administer blood plasma aboard the S.S. Mactan *shortly after it sailed from Manila. When the war began, the military had only 20,000 units of plasma on hand. However, by late January 1942, the weekly average of blood donations for plasma jumped from 1,000 to 5,000 pints, as the American public responded to the surgeon general of the army's "urgent call for blood donors."*

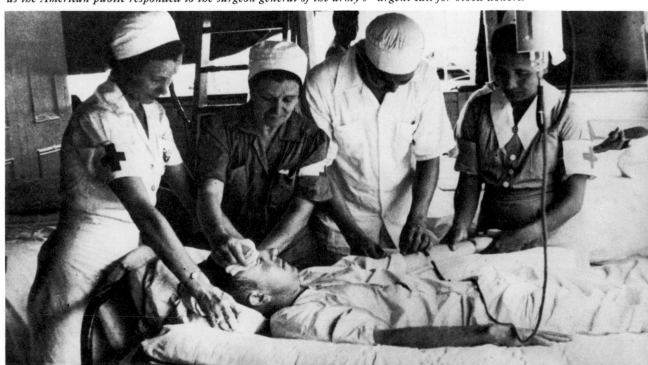

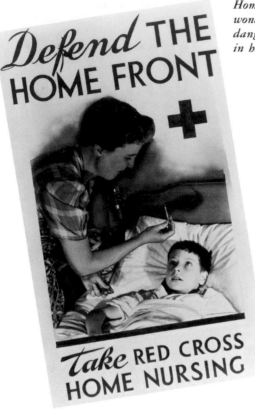

Home nursing grew in popularity during 1942 as Americans wondered which cities would be attacked first. When that danger lessened in 1943, the number of Americans enrolling in home nursing courses dropped off sharply.

The Red Cross machinery, already meeting refugee needs in Europe, smoothly and quickly shifted into action, giving the nation an outlet for service in the face of its frustration over Japan's "dastardly and unprovoked" attack.

The old and the young, the trained and the untrained, donned the Red Cross emblem and started paving the long road to victory.

Mrs. Janette Guttridge, age ninety-three, who did volunteer work during the Civil War, prepares surgical dressings for the Long Beach, California, chapter in 1943.

146

Keyboard sets for practicing the Morse code are assembled by a Junior Red Cross volunteer for the armed forces. The Juniors also made such items as emergency stretchers and traction splints. More than thirteen million youngsters were enrolled in the Junior Red Cross by January 1942, and that enrollment soared to some nineteen million by 1945.

By 1945, 7.5 million volunteers served the nation through the American Red Cross. What makes a good volunteer? "The 'Three Ds'," said Mabel Boardman. *"Drill,* which is her training, *Dependability,* and *Discipline*—the latter being one of the most important, particularly for Americans. The person who is willing to submit to these 'Three Ds,' as I say, makes the best type of volunteer."

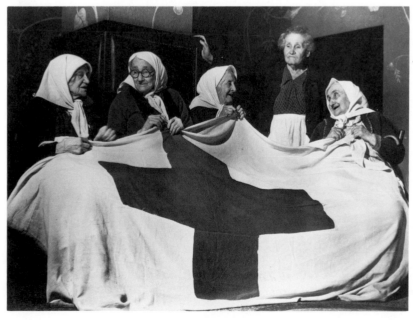

Residents of the Home of Israel, Inc., in New York City, all in their eighties, put the final stitches to a Red Cross flag in January 1942 that will wave from the top of their building.

Publicity hounds. Thirty-five photographers from Lowry Air Force Base converge on volunteer production workers at the Denver Chapter in 1942 to take part in an American Red Cross photography contest.

Retirees and women made up the bulk of the Production Corps with help from the Junior Red Cross. Production Corps volunteers produced 2.5 billion surgical dressings from 1939 to 1946. They also turned out nearly sixteen million "ditty bags" which contained comfort items for the troops and refugees.

Lady with a lamp. During a Washington blackout in March 1942, Daisy Spieler stays at her teletype machine to keep welfare messages flowing to field directors serving the armed forces abroad.

Members of the Wartime Volunteer First Aid Detachment carry "victims" from a simulated boiler explosion in Los Angeles.

Natural disasters took somewhat of a reprieve during the war, but the manmade variety continued to keep chapters busy. Train crashes, chemical plant explosions, and fires which claimed hundreds of lives at public places, such as the Cocoanut Grove nightclub in Boston and the Ringling Brothers and Barnum & Bailey Circus in Hartford, Connecticut.

Rescue workers remove victims of a crash of the Congressional Limited near Philadelphia while a canteen provides hot and cold drinks for them. The train jumped its tracks on September 6, 1943, and hit a tower bridge. Eighty persons died and 125 suffered injuries.

To really involve the whole nation in its work, it was imperative that the Red Cross bring down the racial barriers that prevented minority members from full participation in the war work. The efforts began at the top.

Black leaders gather in the Central Committee Room at national headquarters in one of several meetings held in 1942. Jesse O. Thomas of the Treasury Department, later to become Fieser's special assistant to the director of domestic operations, sits at the extreme left (Fieser is at the head of the table). The meetings were held to give black leaders a chance to advise the administration on what to do about involving the minority more in Red Cross activities. Fieser described the first meeting in July as one punctuated with "bursts of eloquence not found in any of the others which I have attended," starting with "pent up explosiveness and almost bitterness," but eventually giving way to "good humor." The group dealt with issues such as Red Cross personnel policies, blood donations, chapter attitudes, nonrepresentation on boards and committees, and work with enlisted men abroad. "The day in great measure," said Fieser, "was like a surgeon's exploratory incision."

Black leaders chided the American Red Cross for allowing segregation to flourish, especially where blood donations and employment opportunities were involved. The national organization continually sidestepped the issue, insisting that it had no control over local customs and chapter conditions. Realizing the need to actively involve black Americans in its war work, the national headquarters invited black leaders to offer ideas. Their work, combined with the enlightened efforts of a white administrator, soon helped bring about an eventual end of segregation within the Red Cross.

Dean Pickens, a black administrator with the federal government, arose at the first meeting of the Central Committee in 1942 and quickly dismissed any feelings that black Americans had no resolve to fight the Axis powers. Stating that America had given greater opportunity to the Negro than any other country, Pickens added: "If the totalitarian powers got us down, they would give the white man hell and the Negro double hell."

Vice-chairman James L. Fieser, a little-known folk hero within Red Cross national headquarters. He dared to come to grips with the unspoken racial prejudice influencing administrative policies in 1943 when he hired Jesse O. Thomas, a black man, as a special assistant whose main job was to push for minority rights. Although some leaders sympathized with Fieser's motives, few actively supported him in the beginning because of the prevailing indifference to the problem of racial segregation at the highest levels. Some years later, Fieser wrote that "behind our back some called him [Thomas] 'Fieser's Nigger.' He proved invaluable, though Chairman Davis took him on reluctantly."

"No representative of this minority occupied professional status with 95 per cent of the chapters," said black administrator Thomas in 1943, upon being appointed as Fieser's assistant, "with none of the areas, nor on the national staff." Through Thomas's efforts, and Fieser's support of what he was doing, the racial barriers began to crumble.

Operations boomed during World War II. In 1945, over 7.5 million volunteers provided support to nearly 40,000 paid staff around the world. Red Cross personnel followed the invasion forces in Europe and the Pacific, making Service to the Armed Forces the strongest program. Americans showed their support by boosting Red Cross membership to some 37 million regular members and almost 20 million Junior Red Cross members.

General Dwight D. Eisenhower, commander, European Theater of Operations, samples one of the legendary doughnuts at the opening of the Red Cross's Washington Club in London, July 4, 1942. Ike would tell Congress in an address in June 1945: "The Red Cross, with its clubs for recreation, its coffee and doughnuts in the forward areas, its readiness to meet the needs of the well and to help minister to the wounded—even more important, the devotion and warmhearted sympathy of the Red Cross girl! It has often seemed to be the friendly hand of this nation, reaching across the sea to sustain its fighting men."

"Wherever American soldiers gather after this conflict is over," said Vernon Gay, a Red Cross worker at the Rainbow Club, upon its closing in 1946, "they will talk of London, Piccadilly Circus and of Rainbow Corner, and this appreciation will be full reward to the American people for having given their money to the American Red Cross." A Rainbow Club began operating in Paris before the war's end, but it would never replace the London version.

American and British servicemen congregate in front of the Eagle Club, one of the more popular clubs run by the American Red Cross in London in 1942. Perhaps the most popular club was "Rainbow Corner," near Piccadilly Circus, which ran around the clock. At its high point, more than four hundred paid staff and nearly as many volunteers provided food and entertainment for the troops. The service personnel could get a hot meal, a shave and a haircut, back-home conversation with a woman, pinball machines, or just a little time reading in the "quiet room." The Red Cross shared morale-boosting activities with the USO under an agreement reached in March 1942. The Red Cross was responsible for welfare services to active-duty and hospitalized troops, particularly overseas, while the USO was charged with providing "religious, social and recreational activities" to off-duty troops.

Soldiers enjoy a cup of coffee at a Red Cross club in England. When the army asked the Red Cross to set up private clubs overseas for white and black soldiers, the organization asked the advice of black groups. Since the black press was already repudiating the Red Cross for its segregated blood-donating policies, the black spokesmen quickly pointed out that operating segregated clubs overseas would hurt the organization's image internationally. A Red Cross committee of five blacks met and on September 1, 1942, chairman F. D. Patterson, president of Tuskegee Institute, issued a statement that read in part: "clubs patronized largely by Negro soldiers should have a predominantly Negro staff; and those clubs patronized largely by white soldiers should have a predominantly white staff. Both white and Negro personnel should be appointed for all clubs and American soldiers of all races should be welcome at all clubs." The Red Cross adopted the suggested policy immediately. Unfortunately, the troops themselves tended to congregate by race, setting up their own segregation patterns.

Volunteer Eleanor Roosevelt cheers up Australian troops at an American Red Cross club in Australia during her 1943 inspection trip for the organization. Her visit to U.S. military hospitals and American Red Cross facilities brought criticism at home, where Norman Davis defended it as having done "a great deal of good." Columnist Westbrook Pegler wrote from New York that her trip was a junket at the expense of the country and that the Red Cross had "permitted itself to be drawn into politics; and that is bad not only for the Red Cross but for those who, in the end, look to the Red Cross for its service." Pegler reported an army private had been asked by a correspondent on Guadalcanal how he felt about being visited by the President's wife, and the soldier had answered, "I'd rather be visited by my own."

No percolators in the field. A Red Cross clubmobile worker brews up a twenty-five-gallon pot of coffee in England.

A Red Cross field director with the Military Welfare Service prepares to bail out with army paratroopers on maneuvers at Fort Bragg, North Carolina, in November 1943.

Field directors worked and lived with the troops, providing welfare services. They relied on chapters to contact the families of military personnel needing personal and emergency assistance.

By early 1945, the Home Service office in Paris was handling 30,000 cases monthly. Overall, chapter workers handled nearly 18 million cases for service personnel and veterans between 1939 and 1946. Their work entailed the sending of 42 million communications of all types.

Home Service volunteers on night duty at the Danville, Virginia, chapter receive telegrams regarding servicemen overseas. A Home Service worker in Knoxville, Tennessee, in 1944 described the work as "dramatic and fascinating and we believe we are really contributing something to the war effort when we are engaged in this essential Red Cross work." A typical night might include anything from a request for a serviceman's presence due to a family death to the sending of a message abroad that a baby had been born.

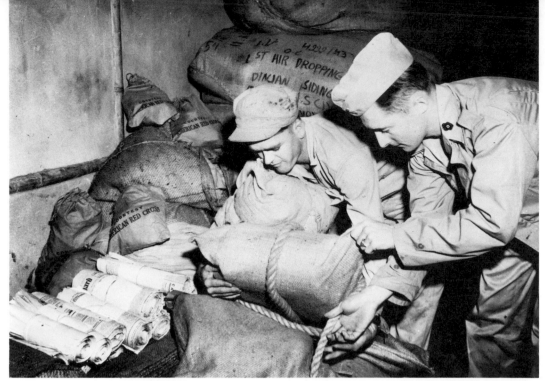

A Red Cross field director and an Army Air Forces crewman prepare to parachute supplies to troops operating in the jungles of Burma in 1944. The supplies included food, newspapers and comfort items. Because of the terrain around the Burma Road, the Red Cross was unable to work close to the front. Instead it operated as far back as 100 miles, running evacuation and field hospitals, on-post clubs, canteens and field director offices. The duty in China, Burma and India proved grueling for staff because of the long hours, the climate and the irregular life they had to lead. Many were sent home for health reasons, and morale was at a low ebb until the organization devised a rotation system in 1944 to send personnel back to the United States for one month's rest.

Chinese coolies guide a sampan loaded with American Red Cross medical supplies down a river in China in 1944, for distribution by field directors dealing with refugees.

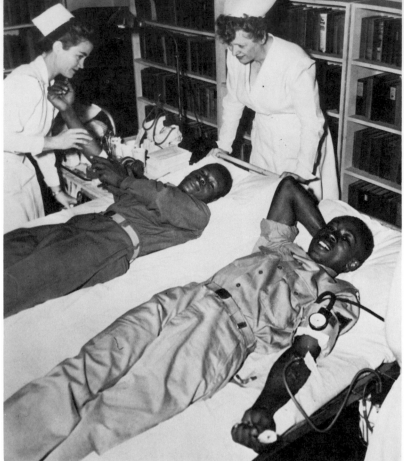

Soldiers donate their blood in Los Angeles. Prior to 1942, blacks were excluded from donating blood to the Red Cross. After January 1942, blacks were allowed to donate blood, but it had to be labeled as to race. Although noting that some people "expected the Red Cross to lead the way to complete equality," chairman Norman Davis in 1942 had the organization follow policies agreed upon with the army and navy surgeons general. "In essence," he said, "it is that we extend all Red Cross relief and services without distinction as to race, but in the detailed conduct of such activities we cannot proceed in a manner which runs counter to the generally accepted wishes and desires of the communities in which the work is conducted." The labeling of blood remained in effect until the Blood Donor Service was phased out at the end of the war.

Shipyard workers from Sparrows Point jam the Red Cross Blood Center in Baltimore, Maryland, signaling the start of a 1943 drive to secure 2,500 pints of blood at the yard.

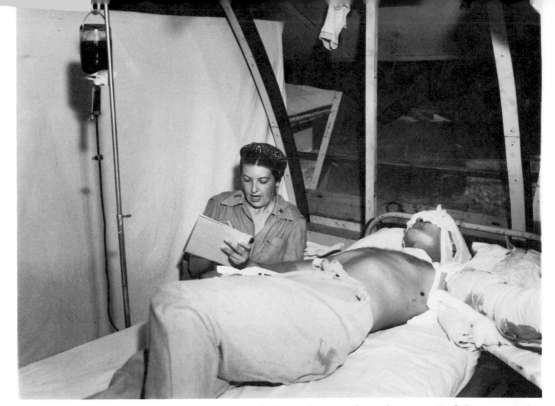

While blood plasma flows into his veins, a wounded man dictates a letter home to a Red Cross recreation worker in the Mariana Islands.

The war effort depended on a steady supply of blood donations. The Red Cross accelerated the work of the Blood Donor Service as plasma needs skyrocketed.

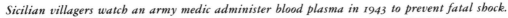

Sicilian villagers watch an army medic administer blood plasma in 1943 to prevent fatal shock.

The invasion of Normandy released an outpouring of blood donations in the United States. In the week of June 5, 1944, a record 123,284 pints of blood were collected for conversion into plasma. Some 25,000 staff and volunteers ran the Blood Donor Service at the peak of its operation in 1944.

A unit of whole blood sent by the American Red Cross to France is used by a nurse at a front-line hospital in Alsace.

Doughnuts became inextricably associated with the American Red Cross in World War II. The organization purchased enough flour between 1939 and 1946 to make 1.6 billion of them. Red Cross women were serving doughnuts at the rate of 400 per minute during the years 1944–46.

Clubmobile women serve coffee and doughnuts to men of a army division manning antiaircraft guns in Italy.

"The Red Cross sold me coffee and doughnuts" became an often repeated complaint following World War II, especially at times when contributions were being solicited. The public relations nightmare stemmed from seemingly innocent government orders at the beginning of the war. Although food and drink in Red Cross domestic canteens were free, the overseas theater was a different matter. Stationary clubs, mainly in Britain, charged a nominal fee for food, lodging, and barber and valet services, at the request of military authorities. Secretary of War Henry Stimson wrote to chairman Davis on May 20, 1942, saying: "The War Department appreciates the motive of the Red Cross with respect to this matter and its established policy of free service, but under the circumstances it is believed impractical, unnecessary, and undesirable that food and lodging be provided for."

Caught in the act? A Red Cross worker sells pastry for five lire to, according to the old photograph caption, "combat troops using the American Red Cross portable tent club" in a Fifth Army area of Italy in 1944. Postwar reports said "no charges were made for articles distributed from mobile facilities such as clubmobiles." Charges were to be levied only "in certain stationary installations such as clubs, as requested by the military." It was debatable whether a portable tent qualified as a stationary facility. The required selling of food created public relations headaches for the Red Cross following the war.

Red Cross clubmobile women refresh the crew of a bomber on a runway in France, using the wing as a shield against a cold rain.

An army corporal gives the "O.K." sign in 1944 after a hot bath at the Red Cross facility at Dijon, France.

A Red Cross hospital worker somewhere in Italy with the U.S. Fifth Army lugs Red Cross materials in a converted Nazi ammunition box.

Hospital workers conducted welfare services and recreation for the wounded at mobile field units and at military hospitals behind the lines and at home.

"Everywhere I went in the European war theater—in the British Isles, in North Africa, and in Sicily—there was the American Red Cross giving its services to our fighting men," wrote war correspondent Ernie Pyle in 1944. "When the Red Cross opens up in a new war theater, its growth has to be as fast as the growth of the Army. The way clubs spring up overnight in newly occupied centers, the way restaurants and dances and movies and clubmobiles and doughnut factories mushroom into life all over a new country, is something that still astonishes me." Pyle died on tiny Ie Shima island off Okinawa while he was covering the fighting there April 18, 1945.

Oh, the rain, the mud, and the cold,
The cold, the mud, and the rain;
With weather at zero it's hard for a hero
From language that's rude to refrain.

from *Rhymes of a Red Cross Man*
Robert W. Service

Red Cross hospital workers attached to a combat unit in Italy in 1943 rough it with the troops.

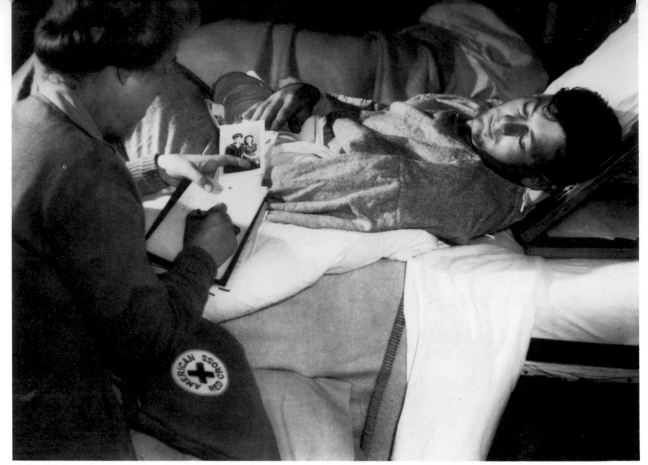

A hospital worker in England writes a letter for a wounded sailor in 1944, while holding a picture of his wife and him. One recreation worker suggested that wives could best help the wounded men when they came home by saying first, "How glad I am to see you!" and then later, "Never mind what has happened to you, you're home now and we'll get over this hump together." Women who do this, she said, "can do more for the men than all the medicine and surgery in the world."

Hospital workers prepare to join a field unit headed for the beaches of Normandy in 1944.

"If I can do it, you can learn too," says Donald Kerr, American Red Cross field director, who jumps onto his artificial leg. Watching are recent amputees at the U.S. Naval Hospital at Mare Island, California, in the closing days of World War II.

Eighty-two decorations were given to Red Cross workers during the war, including three Silver Stars for "gallantry in action." One of those was received posthumously. Richard M. Day of Kirkwood, Missouri, a war correspondent for the Red Cross, was cited for bravery during an invasion in the southwestern Pacific. After the navy coxswain was killed, Day took over the wheel of a landing craft loaded with troops and steered it toward the beach until machine gun fire killed him too. Although twenty-seven of the men were wounded, the craft made it to the beach.

Lieutenant General H. Tamura, chief of the Japanese Prisoner of War Intelligence Bureau, points out locations of internment camps to a U.S. Army colonel in Yokohama, as delegates of the International Red Cross Committee take note. Camp conditions both in Asia and in Europe formed the basis of an extensive report put out by the International Committee of the Red Cross in 1948. It found a wide range of treatment of prisoners. Since Japan had not ratified the Geneva Convention of 1929 which guaranteed protection of prisoners, it felt no obligation to aid prisoners who, under the Bushido code, were without a country because they had surrendered. As a result, few Red Cross packages were allowed, brutality was widespread and disease took a heavy toll of life. The Germans, on the other hand, gave privileged treatment to American, British and French prisoners, while reserving their worst treatment for the Jews, Poles and Russians. Germany was a signatory to the Geneva Convention on prisoners of war; the Soviet Union was not.

Special corps offered men and women volunteers at home a chance to serve in highly identifiable activities that benefited the war effort. Its showing was impressive: the Motor Corps logged more than 60 million miles for the military on convoy and hospital duty; the Canteen Corps prepared nearly 121 million meals for service personnel; and the Production Corps made and repaired articles, numbering in the billions, including surgical items. Then there were the units serving the nation's hospitals, where nurses and others were in short supply—the Nurse's Aide Corps, the Hospital and Recreation Corps, the Dietician's Aide Corps, and the Arts and Skills Corps. Although some felt the corps concept created unnecessary competition, many volunteers were sorry to see the units phased out in the postwar period.

A chapter Gray Lady entertains convalescents at Halloran General Hospital on Staten Island, New York City, in 1945. At the end of the war, nearly 7.5 million volunteers supported Red Cross chapters in various ways, but nearly 6 million had drifted away by 1947, reflecting the nation's return to peacetime concerns.

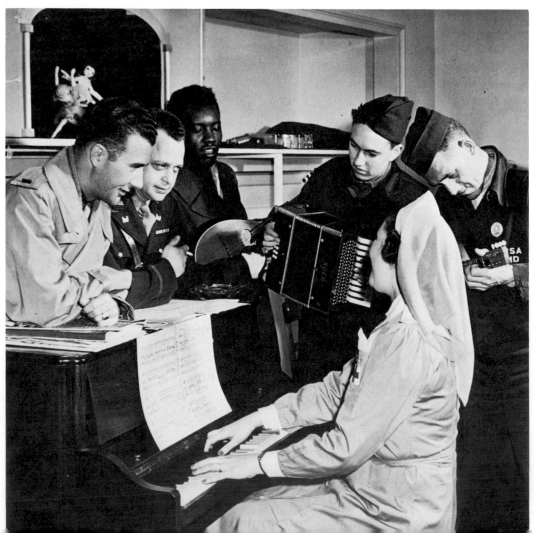

American Red Cross packages for U.S. prisoners at Stalag III B are inspected by Nazi authorities in 1944 under the eye of a delegate from the all-Swiss International Committee of the Red Cross. The camp held 2,800 Americans prisoner, and according to official reports, their main complaints centered around overcrowding, and insufficient heat, light and hot water. The delegate reported that more than three fourths of the prisoners refused to go on work details, a right that the Germans allowed them. U.S. prisoners in France received similar treatment.

Ten million prisoners crowded Axis and Allied prison camps during World War II, giving the Red Cross a huge responsibility. The American Red Cross and its volunteers assembled food packages for 1.3 million Allied and 115,000 American prisoners on behalf of the governments involved. By 1944, ships flying the neutral flag of the Red Cross had carried nearly 26 million packages abroad for distribution to those prisoners.

Standard POW package in 1943. Food packages often provided American prisoners with better fare than their captors had. Red Cross assembly plants in five locations in the East and Midwest provided the prisoners with weekly parcels that supplemented their rations in the camps. The message on the backs of the cigarette packages reads: "Our heritage has always been freedom—we cannot afford to relinquish it—our armed forces will safeguard that heritage if we, too, do our share to preserve it." Special packages for invalids, Christmas packages, and a printed bulletin of nonwar events in the United States were also sent.

Cases of Red Cross packages fill a warehouse in Geneva, Switzerland, prior to their shipment to prisoner of war camps. Working closely with the International Committee of the Red Cross, Red Cross societies were able to arrange the exchange of ill and wounded prisoners, the inspection of prisoner of war camps, and the delivery of mail, food and medical packages.

An American soldier steals a kiss from a surprised Red Cross Motor Corps volunteer on a New York City pier, following his arrival from Europe in May 1945.

The U.S. liberation of Manila saw the headquarters of the American Red Cross Civilian Aid Service besieged daily by throngs of Filipinos seeking assistance of various kinds. The bulk of these are applying for government benefits as dependents of Filipino servicemen.

The war nearly over, a sailor visiting an orphanage in Manila watches a child open a Junior Red Cross package in June 1945.

The war had prepared the Red Cross to meet the needs of the military. When it was over, attention was turned to veterans, the disabled, refugees and war brides.

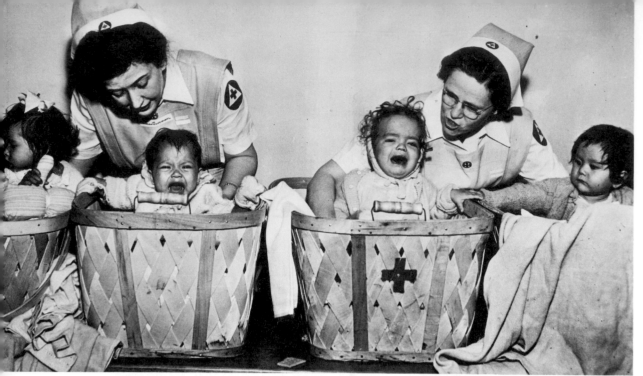

Volunteers of the Nurse's Aide Corps in San Francisco try to cope with the wailing children of internees arriving from the Philippines. The volunteers finally won them over by giving them orange juice, milk and toys—items in short supply in the prison camps. An intensive recruitment campaign swelled the ranks of the Nurse's Aide Corps to nearly 110,000 volunteers by 1943, making it the most successful nursing program. Their main job was to help meet the "emergency needs of the civilian population during the national emergency," which included staffing of hospitals where nursing shortages were acute.

Civilian victims overseas were the greatest tragedy left in the wake of war. The American Red Cross assisted more than 75 million of them between 1939 and 1946. Nearly three million production volunteers at the chapter level produced garments, kits and miscellaneous articles for the war stricken.

Korean youngsters at an orphanage in Inchon, Korea, watch intently as a civilian relief representative for the American Red Cross distributes clothing donated by the people of the United States.

"Stop starvation—tilt the horn of plenty," appealed a Red Cross leaflet in 1946 in response to President Truman's "Famine Emergency" program to end world food shortages. Red Cross chapters called on "victory gardeners and home and community canners to remobilize for an active campaign" on world hunger.

Refugees arriving at Lublin, Poland, in the summer of 1946 are welcomed by Polish Red Cross workers, who will provide them with medical supplies, food and vitamins sent by the American Red Cross. Some two million Poles were returning home after seven years of exile in Siberia.

Werfel's first pair of new shoes. The six-year-old Austrian orphan reacts to shoes provided through the Junior Red Cross in America. His reaction was publicized across the country, sparking a spontaneous outpouring of clothing and other donations for the orphanage in Vienna.

Displaced persons spending Christmas in 1945 in Vienna celebrate with American Red Cross prisoner of war packages left over when hostilities ceased and Axis prison camps were liberated.

War brides brought home by U.S. servicemen learn to shop in an American grocery store with an eye to both nutrition and economy, under the supervision of a Nutrition Service volunteer. The Nutrition Service was dropped as a national program in 1932, but some chapters kept it alive. With World War II, the government asked the Red Cross to instruct Americans in good nutrition. The chapters then launched a "vigorous attack" on the "widespread poor diets and conditions of malnutrition which are weakening the human defense of our democracy," through information booths, classes and discussions on lunchbox nutrition over loudspeakers in factories and shipyards. In 1948, the government began taking over, leading to the discontinuance of the program for the second time.

Junior Red Crossers in Jersey City, New Jersey, pack large educational and health chests which will be sent to war-ravaged parts of the world. The items were paid for by young people throughout the state.

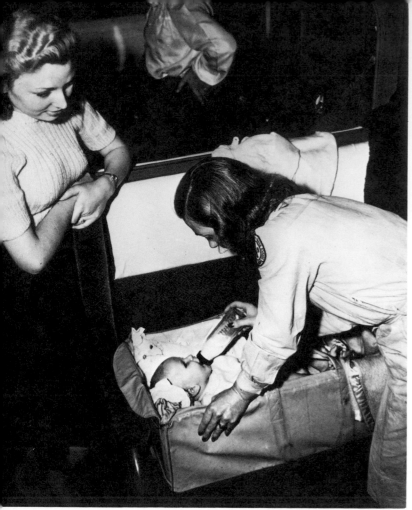

A "war bride train" heads for Chicago from New York in 1946, as a Red Cross volunteer tends the infant of a new arrival from Europe. The volunteers traveled on the trains, providing the weary women with needed assistance.

Mabel Boardman died on March 17, 1946, leaving behind a powerful American Red Cross which she had served faithfully up to within days of her death. She was eighty-five years old. She had retired from her volunteer role as secretary of the Central Committee in December 1944, after receiving the organization's Distinguished Service Gold Medal. "The nation owes you its gratitude," wrote President Roosevelt for the occasion, "for almost 45 years of service to an organization of which the American people are very proud, and have reason to be proud."

6. Going Forward

*P*eace becomes the sought-after goal of Americans in the postwar period. The country struggles to regain normalcy and the Red Cross adjusts its programs accordingly. A revised charter is forthcoming. The blood program is given new life. But then, at a dizzying pace, destiny intrudes again. "Cold war" enters the national vocabulary, and natural disasters take on frightful proportions.

The year 1947 was an important one for the Red Cross. Congress amended the charter to give volunteers a greater role in charting the organization's course, while reaffirming its support for the Red Cross as the best agency to carry out mandates for disaster relief and assistance to the military.

The national convention of that year saw the Red Cross promising the country that it was prepared to "go forward." Chapter delegates hurled challenges from the floor, urging the leadership to confront boldly the nation's pressing problems at home. An overtone of pride regarding past accomplishments shone through, but the message was one of the future, and it was clear. Chapter volunteers would have no more lip service. They demanded that the leadership pave the way with concrete action, because important work lay ahead for the Red Cross.

Emerging from that historic convention was the establishment of a blood program, the largest peacetime project the Red Cross had ever undertaken in the health field. Also making history was the election of thirty chapter delegates to sit on the newly created Board of Governors. For the first time, chapters would have a clear majority on a ruling board, placing the organization's future in the hands of the people who do its work—the volunteers.

The hectic fifties and sixties confronted the organization with a variety of problems stemming from social conditions and economics. Labor disputes, social unrest and chronic unemployment in a comparatively healthy economy forced the Red Cross to take a close look at long-standing policies from another age that mainly restricted it to assisting only in true disaster situations. Fund raising grew more complicated. The last time Red Cross chapters met the national goal was 1949. By 1954, many had begun aligning themselves with outside fund-raising organizations such as United Way, in order to remain effective providers of services.

Dramatic shifts also occurred in the Red Cross attitude toward voluntarism. With the huge numbers of volunteers of World War II suddenly gone, the organization sought to better utilize those still available. That spelled an end to the old separate service corps administered by Mrs. Florence Gardner from 1947–52. A new office to coordinate all volunteer activities was established in 1953. Mrs. Janet Wilson became the first volunteer leader to occupy the post, followed by Mrs. Kay Mills in 1964 and Mrs. Ruth Hildebrand in 1968. Instrumental in that reorganization was E. Roland Harriman.

Harriman, an active volunteer from New York who became Red Cross President in 1950, emerged on the national scene in the immediate post-war period when America's need to return to normalcy caused volunteer strength to slide dramatically. In 1945, at a high-level meeting of volunteers and staff, who sought to revive America's interest in the Red Cross, Harriman had remarked to then President Basil O'Connor: "The trouble with the Red Cross is that it is running around in a 1945 body mounted on a 1905 chassis, with creaks and groans and squeaks." O'Connor agreed and asked Harriman to chair a committee of fifty to study the problem and come up with recommendations to alter it. The study took two years. Its recommendations created a sense of oneness between the national sector and chapters that opened up a new era of Red Cross service in America.

In 1953, Harriman further placed his mark on the organization by restructuring the hierarchy to bring about greater effectiveness. On his recommendation, the Board of Governors changed his title to chairman and elected a full-time, salaried president. During the period, three men would serve in the new presidency—Ellsworth Bunker from 1954 to 1956, General Alfred M. Gruenther, 1957 to 1964, and General James F. Collins, 1964 to 1970. But because of Harriman the chairman, the principal leader of the Red Cross, would always be a volunteer, keeping alive the voluntary spirit upon which the organization was founded.

An occupation soldier hospitalized at the 172nd Station Hospital at Sendai, Japan, in 1947 prepares to put together a leather wallet with help from a recreation worker. During the war, the government began creative rehabilitation programs at military hospitals; the programs led to the formation of the Red Cross Arts and Skills Corps in 1944. Some eleven thousand volunteer artists and craftsmen taught patients how to turn salvage materials into marketable goods. From that time on, handicrafts played a major role in Red Cross hospital recreation programs.

Home nursing courses in the "Land of the Morning Calm." An adviser for the American Red Cross in 1948 instructs a Korean Red Cross nurse who will be teaching in her own country.

A recreation worker in 1947 supervises coconut and bamboo handicraft at Clark Field, Philippines, where Filipino soldiers recover from tuberculosis. They wear masks in an effort to prevent contagion. In 1948, the Philippines Chapter of the American Red Cross became the Philippines National Red Cross, as independence was given to the islands by the United States. Philippines President Roxas signed a national charter incorporating the Red Cross Society on March 22, 1948.

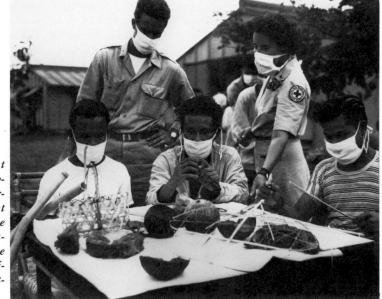

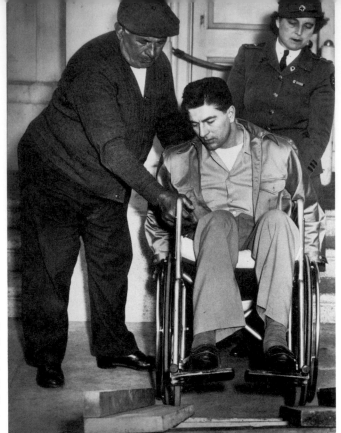

Paraplegic Bernard Cabinese, first graduate of the Bulova Watchmaking School in New York City, is helped onto a special ramp fitted to the back of a Red Cross ambulance with help from a chapter volunteer and a porter at the school. The disabled presented the Red Cross with an important rehabilitation role, one providing great satisfaction to the volunteers.

President Truman signs an amended congressional charter May 8, 1947, giving the American Red Cross a landmark document, as Chairman Basil O'Connor and Howard Bonham, vice-chairman in charge of public relations, look on. The charter gave local chapters greater representation in the management and control of the whole organization than they had ever had before. The Central Committee was abolished and replaced by a Board of Governors, numbering fifty. Eight of the members were to be picked by the U.S. President, the honorary chairman of the organization; twelve members were to be selected by the board itself, and the remaining thirty members were to be elected by the local chapters at the national convention. In addition, anyone in the United States could be a member of the Red Cross for a fee of one dollar annually.

"I am well aware this year's [Red Cross] convention is an historic one as I had the privilege of signing the bill which the Congress had passed unanimously authorizing vital changes in our charter."

Harry S. Truman
Letter to Basil O'Connor
June 9, 1947

First day on the job. General George C. Marshall (right) accompanies new president E. Roland Harriman up the steps at national headquarters on December 4, 1950. Harriman, a banker and railroad executive, would serve in an unpaid capacity for twenty-three years. Marshall, who succeeded O'Connor as president in 1949, had resigned after being named Secretary of Defense.

Trying for a repeat of 1949, the last year that the Red Cross exceeded its financial goal nationally, the organization enlists the help of the Goodyear blimp to begin its 1950 campaign in Miami.

After two years of dormancy, the Red Cross revived its blood program in response to the proddings of doctors who were trying to meet shortages at the hospital level. It would be the largest peacetime undertaking in the health field in the organization's history. And it would be an unqualified success.

Representatives from various civic groups await the arrival of Red Cross President Basil O'Connor for the dedication of the first blood center under the new blood program on January 12, 1948 at Rochester, New York. Within eighteen months, centers were spread across a twenty-state area. The Red Cross Board of Governors approved the revival of a national blood program in June 1947 after surveys revealed that only about 20 percent of the nation's hospitals had blood banks. Leaders of the American Medical Association and other health groups had urged the American Red Cross to start the national blood program.

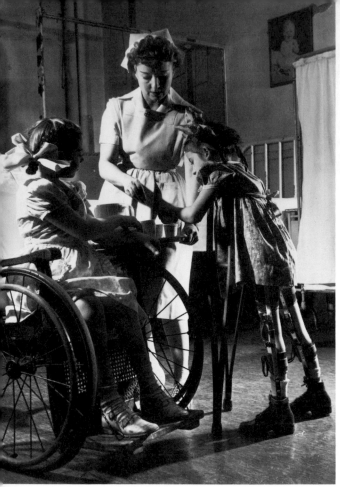

A Red Cross volunteer, one of some twelve thousand volunteer nurse's aides who served in hospitals in 1948, works with two victims of infantile paralysis at Children's Hospital in Washington. The Red Cross also fought the crippling disease by making its nurses available for duty during polio epidemics through an agreement with the National Foundation for Infantile Paralysis. Epidemics in America were at their worst from 1942 to 1953.

Through sustained efforts by various health agencies, including the Red Cross, the leg braces and iron lungs that followed the summer scourges of polio became a thing of the past as new vaccines made their appearance.

A doctor administers a shot of serum globulin during field trials in 1952 aimed at seeing if the injections provoked a greater incidence of polio during an epidemic. They didn't. Serum globulin, a derivative of human blood collected by the American Red Cross, helped cut the incidence of polio cases in the early 1950s. Salk vaccine appeared in 1955, greatly reducing polio outbreaks. But the real breakthrough was the oral vaccines which were introduced in America in the early sixties. They virtually eradicated the disease by making the inoculated population epidemic proof.

178

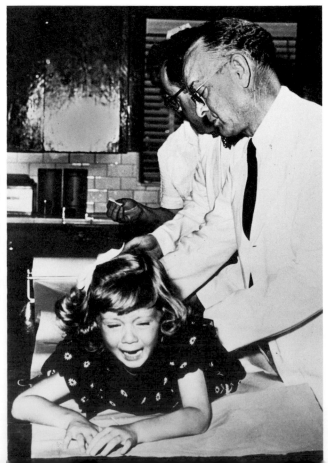

With America again sending its men abroad to fight, Red Cross blood centers around the country produced a constant supply of blood for plasma. According to a publicity manual for the government's National Blood Program, "Plasma, the fluid part of your blood, is actually about 92 percent water. Only 7 percent of it is proteins, which do amazing things for you. Plasma also contains a small amount of sugar, fat, salt, and other minerals."

"The giving of blood is imbued with the psychology of peace, for it leaves its humanitarian mark in the hearts of those who give for their fellowmen."

Red Cross Courier
July 1947

Communist North Korea invaded South Korea on June 25, 1950, triggering the first cold war conflict involving U.S. troops. The American Red Cross again pledged volunteers, blood and expanded programs to help an America rapidly moving onto a war footing.

With the outbreak of hostilities in Korea, General Douglas MacArthur requested that the American Red Cross expand its traditional services and add on a recreation club system, which had been turned over to Army Special Services during the period 1947–48. This put the Red Cross in a significant position to give service not only to American troops, but to all United Nations forces. By 1953, the small club system had been replaced by a highly mobile recreation force, whose women traveled to the front lines to bolster the morale of the troops.

179

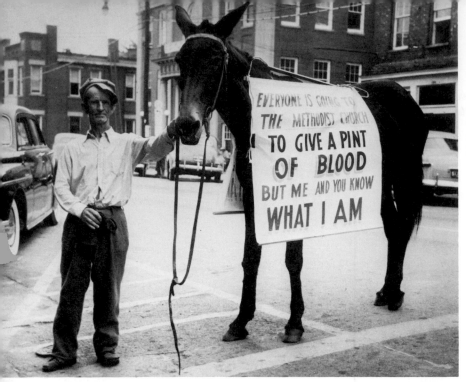

A volunteer uses his mule to make his views known while the Red Cross bloodmobile visits Lebanon, Kentucky, in the early days of the Korean War.

"This is the first time in our history where we have had to fight during the first week of a war. Not only does the Red Cross have to gather fresh whole blood for the wounded in the Far East, but it is involved in a tremendous program of stockpiling blood plasma for civilian defense needs."

General George C. Marshall
Red Cross President

"During those two terrible days in November when wounded and frozen members of the 7th Infantry Division were being rescued across the ice of the Chosin Reservoir by men from the 1st Marine Regiment, there was one of their number who refused to be evacuated. Once rescued, he dragged other men to safety from under the fire of Chinese snipers, only 150 yards away. Lost in admiration of this performance, the Marines wanted to decorate him. He said: 'I'm supposed to do this work; I'm the Red Cross man with the 7th Division.'"

Colonel Marshall
Letter to the Editor
Detroit News, March 1951
(excerpted)

A jeep hood serves as a desk for two soldiers talking to a Red Cross field director (left) in 1950.

Over the years there have been frequent complaints such as, "The Red Cross wouldn't let me go home when my father died." The Red Cross has unsuccessfully tried to explain since World War II that only commanding officers can grant emergency leave. The Red Cross, through its many chapters, merely verifies the facts upon which the commanding officer's decision is sometimes made.

Concern about home conditions could have devastating effect on the morale of troops at the front. A quick request through the military communications system to the local Red Cross chapter ended the suspense. Either the man was assured all was well or the stage was set for further action to resolve the problem. Rapid telecommunications could bring messages back in a day or two, but getting the word to a line soldier on the move at the front could sometimes take weeks, a frustrating situation for both the man and the Red Cross worker.

"While the day to day work of the Field Directors of the divisions is quiet and undramatic, the soldier in the line has learned to look to the Red Cross for assistance in the solution of many of his pressing problems."

Gen. Matthew B. Ridgway
United States Army
(following a visit to the Korean front
in May 1951)

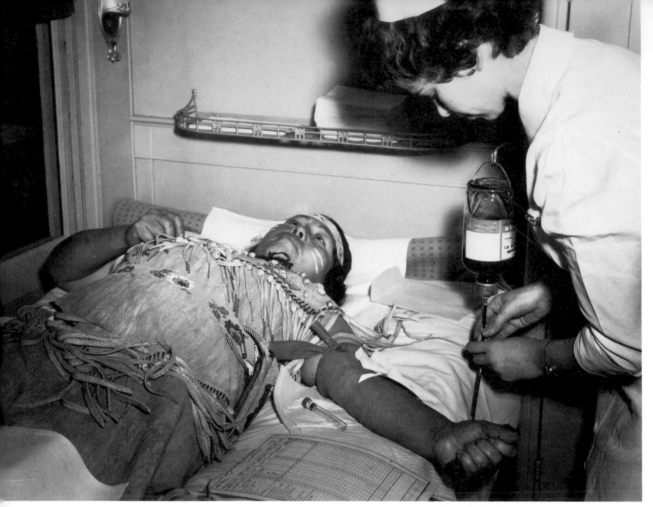

An Indian woman taking part in ceremonies at Elko, Nevada, gives blood aboard a procurement railroad car, named Charles O. Sweetwood after the first employee of the Nevada and Western Pacific Railroad to die in the Korean War. The car was equipped to handle four donors at a time. It also contained sleeping quarters for the staff and an examining room. The Korea situation forced an end to subtle discrimination which existed after 1947 in some communities where Red Cross blood collections were performed. On September 10, 1950, the Committee on National Blood Program of the Board of Governors approved the following motion: "That racial designation on donor cards should be withdrawn and that where the doctors find need for surveys for scientific purposes, that the facilities of the National Blood Program be made available to them so that they could gather the required information."

President Truman established a federal blood program on December 10, 1951, to bring about an "integrated and effective program to meet the nation's requirements for blood, blood derivatives and related substances." The executive order, which coincided with escalating fighting in Korea, designated the Red Cross as "the blood collecting agency for the defense needs of the National Blood Program." To avoid confusion with the government program, the Red Cross stopped referring to its own blood service as a "national" one, and simply called it the "American Red Cross Blood Program."

Searching the skies for evacuation helicopters, United Nations soldiers, including Americans, Turks and South Koreans, transfuse the "gift of life" into the wounded following a major battle in 1952. The American Red Cross collected 2.5 million pints for the military in that year, but a severe shortage of blood still persisted. At the time, the armed forces were requiring 300,000 pints of blood monthly.

A badly wounded American soldier receives a pint of blood before being evacuated to a rear area of Korea in 1951. The use of helicopters and improved medical techniques drastically reduced the mortality rate in Korea. According to the Department of Defense, "Only 2.6 patients out of every hundred reaching the most forward hospitals subsequently died." That was almost 50 percent lower than World War II, when plasma was impressively reducing death from shock.

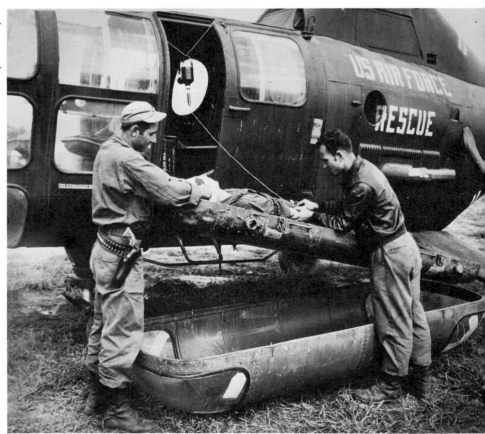

The men of the carrier U.S.S. Boxer *form a blood bottle on the flight deck of their ship after a record-breaking donation in October 1951. The 2377 stands for the number of pints they donated during a three-day period. From 1950 to 1953, the Red Cross collected and procured nearly five million pints of blood for the armed forces.*

A clubmobile worker fills her mug with coffee while standing a two-hour fire watch over the stoves heating the Red Cross billet in Korea. The women who carried recreation to the troops in the field were college graduates with good grades who were selected for the short-term duty because of their leadership potential. It took special skills to organize activities for groups of men numbering as many as 250 at times. The women organized games, sketching groups, handicrafts, group singing, and the like. They found the average American serviceman to be a bright and knowledgeable participant who taxed their ability to come up with creative activities. The main problems facing the young women were boredom, isolation and lack of public appreciation for the sacrifices they were making. Unlike the USO and Special Services Clubs, the Red Cross conducted the recreational activities during on-duty hours to give line troops a much-needed break. Facing a diminished need for the Supplemental Recreational Activities Overseas program at the end of the Vietnam War, the organization terminated it in June 1973.

GI's sweating out rotation transportation back to the United States mingle with French troops (berets) at the Red Cross club at Camp Mower, in Sasebo, Japan. Lines half a mile long were common. The Red Cross ran similar clubs in Korea, but phased them out in favor of a new program in August 1953 that concentrated on smaller centers and the sending of teams of recreation workers into the field. Under the Supplemental Recreational Activities Overseas program, the women traveled by military transportation to forward and isolated areas daily to provide on-duty recreation for the often demoralized troops. Ten such units operated at the program's peak. Doughnuts played a minor role under the reorganization.

Saving face, an important element in negotiations in the Orient, caused considerable delay during cease-fire talks at Panmunjom between the Communist forces and the United Nations forces. Casualties soared during the two years of cease-fire and armistice talks. On December 11, 1951, the negotiators tackled the last item on their agenda, prisoners of war, but it would be 1953 before prisoner of war exchanges could be rearranged. On July 27, 1953, the armistice ending the Korean War was signed, setting the stage for the release of prisoners. The actual exchange began August 5.

James Nicholson, executive vice-president and general manager of the American Red Cross, makes a point during talks at Panmunjom with Korean Red Cross representatives, aimed at making the exchange of prisoners go smoothly in August 1953. Operation Big Switch would take six weeks to complete. George M. Elsey, assistant to Nicholson and former administrative assistant to President Truman, sits in the far left corner. In May 1953, Operation Little Switch occurred, involving the exchange of about eight thousand sick and wounded prisoners.

A United Nations soldier arriving at Freedom Village on the 38th parallel in Korea is greeted by an American Red Cross field director serving on a joint Red Cross team that dealt with the exchange of prisoners of war. Operation Big Switch began on August 5, 1953, marking a true end of hostilities in Korea. Almost 12,000 prisoners were sent back by the Communists. Most of the non-Koreans were reported as being in "reasonably good physical condition although many bore the impress of strain." However, nearly 50 percent of the South Korean prisoners suffered from tuberculosis, many in advanced stages. The UN side returned more than 75,000 prisoners to the Communist side.

Revolution swept Hungary in 1956. The League of Red Cross Societies called on the American Red Cross for help, and a massive relief effort was mustered to help Hungarian refugees trying to escape their Soviet-dominated land.

A Hungarian Red Cross truck creeps up a street in Budapest in search of casualties, November 1, 1956, during the temporary withdrawal of Soviet troops. A revolutionary armed with a rifle sits on the fender to ensure the safety of the Red Cross personnel. Eight days earlier, students took to the streets to protest the Soviet presence in their country, toppling Stalin's statue and battling Russian tanks with rocks and firebombs. Shortly after, the League of Red Cross Societies stepped in to begin coping with the needs of the Hungarians. The Red Cross was soon joined by CARE, the World YMCA, the International Union for Child Welfare, and other voluntary relief agencies.

Red Cross workers on the Austrian side of the Austro-Hungarian frontier use a coat and flag to signal refugees attempting to cross the border on foot in November 1956. Other escapees stand in the background. About six thousand refugees streamed across the border daily, most of them males between the ages of eighteen and thirty-five who had been involved in the uprising. The American Red Cross operated four of the largest refugee centers in Austria.

At Idlewild Airport, New York. Monsignor Bela Varga, president of the Hungarian National Council, blesses medical supplies destined for riot victims in Budapest. The International Committee of the Red Cross later refuted charges in the U.S. that Soviet troops had intercepted medical supplies, removed their Red Cross markings and sold them on the black market. The committee reported that "none of our columns met with any difficulties."

The end of an ordeal. An embrace and tears mark a meeting between a refugee and his relative (wearing hat), already living in the United States. The Red Cross worked closely with government agencies and others at Camp Kilmer, New Jersey, where a reception center had been set up. The organization assisted some thirty thousand refugees at the center, and shipped nearly seven hundred tons of medical and other supplies overseas to refugee camps in Austria and to Hungary itself. The U.S. center closed down May 15, 1957, but the work went on. The Red Cross assisted about eight hundred refugees monthly from an office at the St. George Hotel in Brooklyn, where they could obtain clothing, comfort articles and welfare services.

The cold war resulted in American civilians being detained in China. "Having no material way to express my gratitude," wrote a priest who was allowed his first Red Cross package in 1955 after nine years of imprisonment, "I would rather quote: 'I was hungry, and you gave me to eat; I was thirsty and you gave me to drink . . . I was in prison and you came to me.'"

"It is a source of great satisfaction that the Red Cross was able to bring about the freeing of these men and return them safely to their families," said General Alfred M. Gruenther, president of the American Red Cross, on July 19, 1958, as nine U.S. helicopter crewmen were freed by the East Germans. The American Red Cross negotiated the release through the East German Red Cross, bringing about their freedom some forty-three days after their aircraft strayed across the border in bad weather.

The Red Cross flag aboard the freighter S.S. Morning Light captures the dawn's rays on May 24, 1963, the day it arrived with 751 refugees from the Castro regime. All told, nine ships and thirty-six planes ferried supplies and refugees during the operation, which was monitored by the government but was strictly out of its hands. The effort was a voluntary one, with businesses, airline and trucking companies, insurance firms, shipping outfits and labor unions donating their services without charge.

"As I came out of the prison in Havana yesterday," said a released prisoner of Brigade 2506, "I could see the ship coming into the harbor. I saw the red crosses on her side, and I knew this was the ship that meant my life and my family." The United States Post Office Department issued a commemorative stamp with a 5¢ denomination during the period October 26–29, 1963, to honor the centenary of the International Red Cross. The photograph below was the subject of the stamp.

"Through our relationship with sister societies around the world, the American Red Cross is able to hurdle the differences between nations to carry on its humanitarian services," said president Alfred Gruenther.

The abortive Bay of Pigs invasion by Cuban exiles in April 1961 set the stage for the American Red Cross to carry out a truly humanitarian mission with the Cuban Red Cross, helping the Cuban Families Committee arrange the release of the men and their relatives. In return, Cuba received donated children's food and medical supplies amounting to $53 million between December 1962 and July 1963. U.S. Attorney General Robert Kennedy, whose Justice Department had asked the organization to become involved, "paid warm tribute" and "voiced the view that the Red Cross' activities saved the lives of the 1,113 prisoners."

Overcome with emotion, a Cuban woman arriving at Port Everglades, Florida, aboard the Morning Light *has her blood pressure checked before debarking. She was one of 7,857 relatives of the released prisoners who eventually found new homes in America. Red Cross doctors checked all elderly people before they were allowed to get off the ship. Hundreds of Red Cross volunteers were on hand, distributing comfort items to the prisoners, manning canteens, assisting the newcomers with transportation and temporary housing arrangements, and rendering nursing services.*

A police officer at Bridgeport, Connecticut, attempts to revive a drowned youth in July 1956 with the back pressure/arm lift method of artificial resuscitation. The technique was adopted in 1951 by the Red Cross but dropped in favor of the more effective mouth-to-mouth resuscitation in 1959 after it was successfully used on children for nearly two years. Although new to the Red Cross, the technique could be traced back to Biblical times, when Elisha revived the Shunammite woman's child, as related in Chapter 4 of the Second Book of Kings: "And he went up, and lay upon the child, and put his mouth upon his mouth, and his eyes upon his eyes, and his hands upon his hands: and he stretched himself upon the child; and the flesh of the child waxed warm."

Members of a Red Cross canoeing class lock hands over the bottom of a capsized canoe to remain above water without undue effort. Boating students are taught to stay with their capsized craft because it generally will remain afloat. The Red Cross Small Craft program was formalized in 1952, and in 1956 the first canoeing textbook was published.

Rescuers administer mouth-to-mouth resuscitation to a storm victim in New York City. Ten-foot tides, the highest up to that time, swept into the city's streets, setting homes awash following the onslaught of Hurricane Donna in 1960.

Chapter volunteers kept the Red Cross before the public by providing free service that saved the nation millions of dollars.

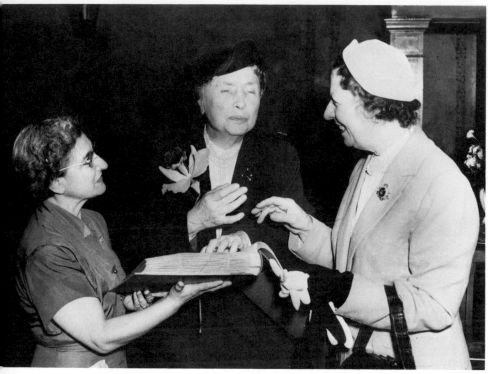

Author–fund raiser Helen Keller, blind and deaf since childhood, visits the Newark Chapter in 1952 and is presented with a special braille book put together in commemoration of her tour of its Braille Department. One of the most active braille centers in the nation, the Newark Red Cross service was first organized in 1933. In 1945, it had 106 volunteers, 76 of whom were certified transcribers. During the war years, they gave nearly 55,000 hours of service that brought books, radio scripts, first-aid manuals, knitting instructions, playing cards, and other items to the nation's blind, especially newly disabled veterans.

The gift of self. A volunteer for the Atlanta, Georgia, chapter serves at an outpatient clinic at Grady Memorial Hospital, looking after infants while their mothers are being treated. Voluntarism is one of the few fields that know no age barriers.

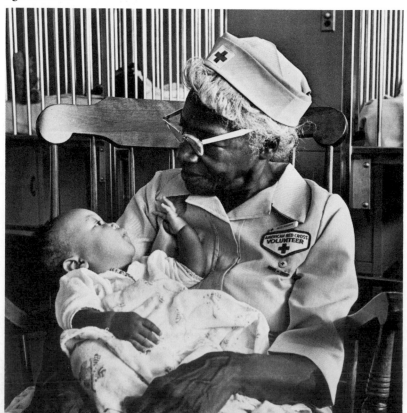

Survival of the Red Cross depended on two important elements—public support through voluntary service and contributions and development of future leaders from the vast pool of American youth. A major study in 1956 revealed that many young people thought of the Junior Red Cross as "a sissy organization" and "mostly for girls." They also thought adult leaders were too "paternalistic" and at times "too rigid" regarding their role. The survey indicated that young people wanted "adult type" roles and "more significant projects" to work on. Efforts then got under way to bring about greater involvement of American youth, but the decline in membership continued. In October 1964, the name of the service was changed to Red Cross Youth in an attempt to overcome the reluctance of young people to be categorized as "juniors" and in hope of reversing the trend.

A Junior Red Cross hospital volunteer aids an airman at the American Air Force hospital in Wiesbaden, Germany, in 1962. Forty high school students helped out at the hospital that summer in jobs ranging from working in the pharmacy to working on the hospital wards. Young people in the sixties preferred adult-type duties to the structured "Friendship Boxes" and other long-standing tasks that grownups were uninterested in.

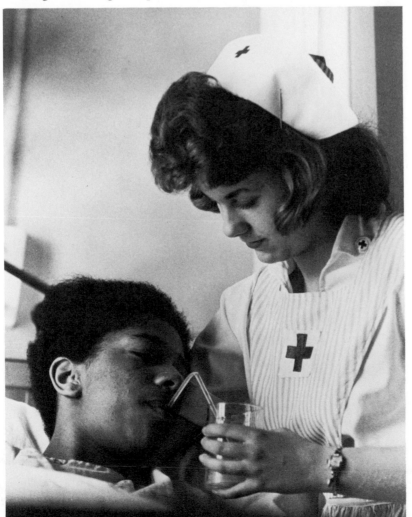

A chapter volunteer receives a spontaneous hug from a retarded child at Camp Kentan, Virginia, in April 1964. Five Virginia chapters carefully selected and trained 100 teen-agers to serve as counselors during the four weeks the camp for the mentally retarded was in operation near Middleburg, Virginia. Red Cross chapters have made a concentrated effort since the early 1960s to reach the physically and mentally handicapped, seeing the work as meaningful public service.

An American volunteer with a Friendship Mexico project tries to console a woman in a Mexican hospital who has lost a loved one. In a demonstration of the new direction the Red Cross Youth program was trying to take, fifty U.S. college students served in twenty Mexican communities in 1967, training instructors and conducting classes in first aid, water safety, home nursing and baby care.

A Red Cross Youth volunteer rocks a child at St. Michael's Day Nursery in Wilmington, Delaware, in the summer of 1969. Approximately 350 other high school and college students from the Wilmington chapter spent their summers giving service in hospitals, nursing homes and day nurseries that year.

The fifties became known as the "decade of disasters" as both manmade and natural calamities struck with awesome force, depleting Red Cross disaster funds and exacting great sacrifices of lives and money from the American people. From 1949 to 1959, the organization handled no fewer than 3,100 major relief operations.

Natural disasters sent chapters scurrying to meet the needs of victims from one coast to the other.

197

Volunteers hurriedly help families escape the heavy seas battering Misquamicut, Rhode Island, as Hurricane Carol approaches in the summer of 1954. Nearly twelve thousand families in New England and Long Island were affected as the storm strained the capacities of Red Cross chapters serving the area. Shelters for the homeless were set up, and food, clothing, and medical and nursing care were provided.

THE TIMES-PICAYUNE, NEW ORLEANS, SEPT. 12, 1961

A Louisiana newspaper shows the appreciation felt by New Orleans citizens who were helped by the Red Cross in the aftermath of Hurricane Carla in 1961.

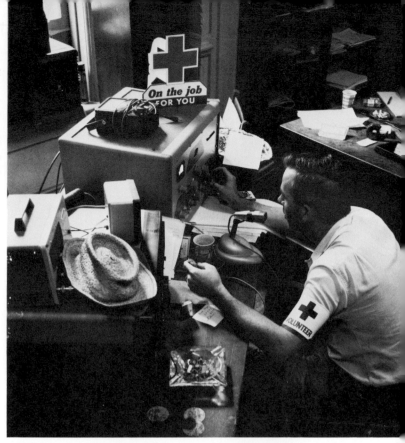

Ham radio operators play a key role in the American Red Cross disaster structure. A chapter volunteer maintains an all-night vigil at Key West, Florida, during Hurricane Donna's passage through the area in 1960, directing rescuers to people in distress and monitoring various emergencies.

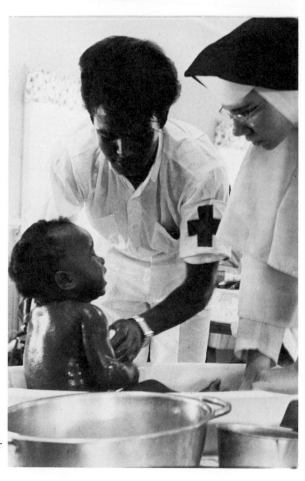

Red Cross volunteers bathe a baby, one of the many refugees who sought assistance in Red Cross shelters in New Orleans following the onslaught of Hurricane Betsy in September 1965.

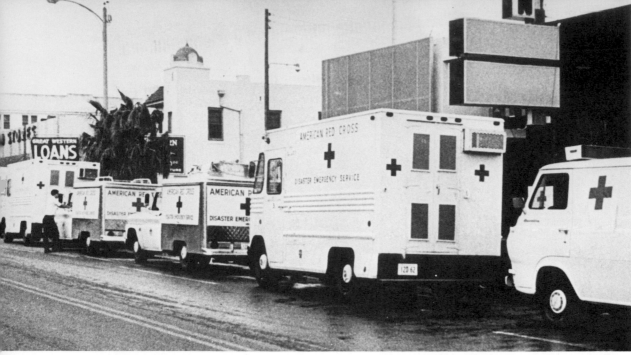

Mobile feeding vans and canteens line up for cargoes of hot food that will be served to the victims of Hurricane Beulah in 1967.

Modern disaster techniques include giving victims redeemable vouchers that can be used at the stores of their choice. In addition to avoiding the logistical problems involved in collecting donated clothing, the vouchers stimulate business and thus benefit the merchants in the disaster areas, a necessary step in helping communities recover. These posters in Biloxi, Mississippi, were also placed in other communities affected by Hurricane Camille in August 1969.

Tornadoes sweeping through the Oklahoma and Texas Panhandle area leave their mark in the spring of 1947. The storm systems struck five times between April 9 and May 31. Hundreds of Red Cross volunteers rushed in to provide mass housing, food and medical attention, and they were quickly followed by damage surveyors and other rehabilitation specialists. The storms left 165 dead and more than 1,000 injured. Woodward, Oklahoma, alone lost 91 residents as blocks of homes were demolished. "In the ghastly night," wrote one newsman, "lit only by fires in the shattered wreckage, half-stunned hysterical people staggered through the blinding rain and the snow that followed."

Tornadoes raked America from the East Coast across the Midwest to the Southwest in the fifties and sixties, killing hundreds and destroying millions of dollars' worth of property.

A volunteer tenderly wipes the face of a victim amid the rubble of her home following a tornado that roared through Worcester, Massachusetts, June 9, 1953. More than two thousand families suffered loss in the tornado and seventy-nine persons were killed. Red Cross disaster specialists and volunteers by the hundreds pitched in to help.

A Junior Red Cross volunteer nails a poster to a telephone pole to alert the residents of Lexington, Tennessee, that shelter, food and medical care are available at the local National Guard armory.

Water thunders down a street in Putnam, Connecticut, washing over a bridge and into the city. "The Awful Flood of 1955," is what the Hartford, Connecticut, Times called the disaster in its August 26 edition. The eastern states floods began in Pennsylvania on August 18 and rapidly moved into New England, with waters that sometimes swelled to forty feet above flood stage. The flooding, triggered by back-to-back hurricanes Connie and Diane, killed some 184 people in a two-week period beginning August 7.

Volunteers take nourishment after fortifying dikes with sandbags at Council Bluffs, Iowa, as floodwaters threaten to crest in April 1952.

"It rained and rained and rained and then the floods came," said a report on the eastern states floods of 1955. The flooding prompted the Red Cross to describe all previous disasters as "a dress rehearsal" in comparison. President Eisenhower urged Americans to dig deeply into their pockets to enable the Red Cross "to meet this great disaster that has happened to our fellow Americans." At the height of the disaster, the Red Cross was running 131 shelters in six states, with thousands of the victims remaining there for as long as a month.

In 1957, an editorial cartoonist for the Cincinnati Enquirer *calls the Red Cross the "Rock of Ages."*

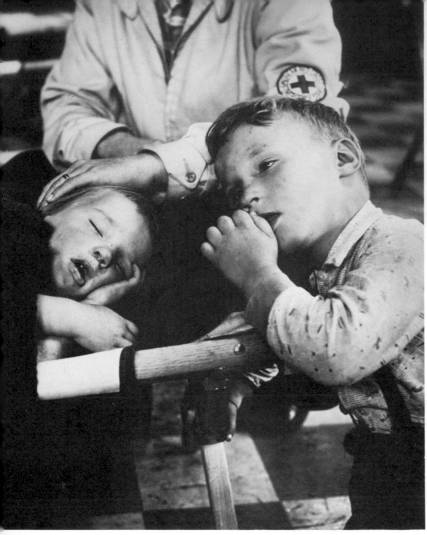

Two tired children at a Red Cross shelter are relieved of tension and anxiety caused by flooding of their home in Valley Park, Missouri, in May 1961. The floods inundated counties in a five-state area of the Midwest. Complicating matters was a spate of tornadoes that struck thirty counties at the same time. The Red Cross fed or sheltered more than three thousand victims and provided food for an additional six thousand emergency workers who were trying to keep levees from collapsing.

The Mudgett Bridge at Rio Dell, California, in December 1964, following heavy flooding.

Volunteers clean up the basement of an elderly resident's home following the Montana-Idaho floods of June 1964. Red Cross teams of two to five volunteers daily visited homes of the handicapped, the elderly and the widowed to remove mud and debris.

Earthquakes, in their unpredictable deadliness, caused unestimable tragedy.

Good Friday 1964. The earth shook violently and buildings collapsed in minutes when an earthquake hit the Anchorage, Alaska, area on March 27, killing 115 persons and causing millions of dollars of damage. Red Cross teams rushed in to provide food, shelter and clothing in coordination with other relief agencies and the government. Shortly afterward, Congress passed legislation making funds available to pay off mortgages still owed by many of the victims. That marked the beginning of more involvement by the government in the costly rehabilitation phase of disaster work, which eventually allowed the Red Cross to ease out of long-term relief and concentrate on the emergency periods.

An American Red Cross field director at Andrews Air Force Base, Maryland, in July 1963, checks bales of blankets being airlifted by the Air Force for the relief of Yugoslavian earthquake sufferers. The Red Cross supplies also included drugs and medicines, clothing and children's educational, recreational and comfort materials. The organization responded to appeals from the League of Red Cross Societies, which rallies national societies whenever a country is unable to handle a disaster entirely on its own.

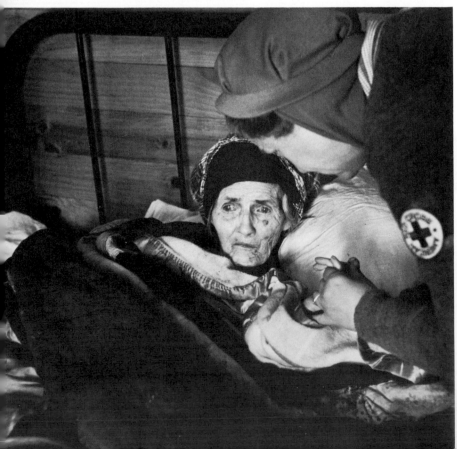

A woman in her eighties is finally attended to by a volunteer nurse after being marooned for about three weeks following a March snowstorm in the North Carolina mountains in the late 1960s.

Army vehicles provided the Red Cross with the help it needed to rescue the snowbound in the North Carolina mountains. Some of the more seriously ill people had to be flown out by helicopter in one of the more unusual disasters involving the Red Cross.

Ship collisions and fires drew the Red Cross into action.

The Italian liner **Andrea Doria** *lies on its side as it begins to sink some forty-five miles south of Nantucket Island on July 26, 1956. Late the night before, the ship collided with the Swedish liner* **Stockholm** *in thick fog, leaving about fifty persons dead or missing.*

Dazed survivors of the collision recount their tale of the hectic minutes before they climbed into lifeboats to escape the damaged **Andrea Doria**. *Most of the survivors left all possessions behind.*

A Red Cross nurse cradles a survivor on a New York pier. The New York Chapter provided clothing, food, cash and transportation for the survivors, and set up a system to handle health and welfare inquiries from worried relatives.

Father and daughter burst into tears as their home burns to the ground at Upper Merion, Pennsylvania. American Red Cross involvement with fires and small disasters kept chapters busy across the nation. Before 1964, "five or more families" was the guideline for providing disaster relief. A resolution passed at the 1964 national convention eliminated the long-established rule, as it had become apparent that a great need existed for Red Cross assistance in situations with less than national scope.

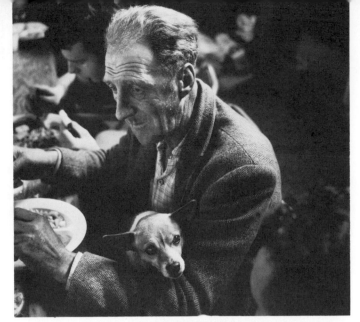

The aftermath of disaster has many faces.

The Vietnam War divided Americans into "hawk" and "dove" camps. But where captured American prisoners were concerned, there was more willingness to unite. The North Vietnamese refused to honor the 1949 Geneva Convention ensuring adequate protection of prisoners of war. At the International Conference of the Red Cross in Istanbul, Turkey, in 1969, the American Red Cross and the U.S. government cosponsored a resolution asking all nations to renew their pledge to the principles of the Geneva Convention. It was adopted without dissent. "This is a matter that has nothing to do with the wisdom of U.S. policies in Vietnam," said U.S. Senator George McGovern. "No American, irrespective of his views on the war, can condone the North Vietnamese handling of prisoners of war."

A male nurse at Binh Son, South Vietnam, examines a youngster at one of forty-five camps meeting the needs of refugees in October 1968. An all-male team of ten American Red Cross specialists provided various services for the tens of thousands of refugees who flooded the camps during the war. Camp personnel offered instruction in rudimentary hygiene, provided social welfare services and made medical assistance available. They also involved the refugees in self-help projects in carpentry, masonry and sanitation, and gave them the tools to work with.

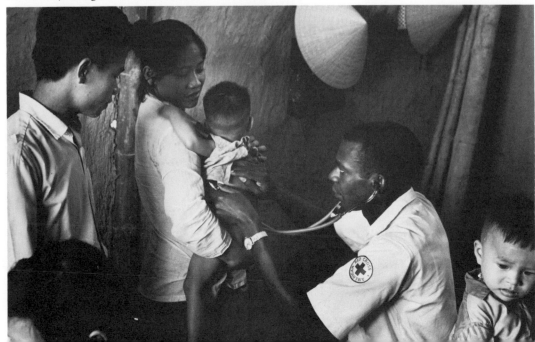

Youngsters work on an American Red Cross youth friendship project for the needy children in war-torn Vietnam. They packed toothbrushes, paste, soap, toys and other items for the children. Tens of thousands of similar kits and boxes were shipped to Southeast Asia during the war.

"Brush in tiny circles for healthy teeth and gums" is the message from an American Red Cross worker to these refugee children at a camp in Quang Ngai, South Vietnam.

Fire Support Base Nashua provides a silhouette in 1967 that belies its hostile mission in Vietnam. The Red Cross first sent field staff to Vietnam in 1962 to assist the growing number of servicemen with emergent and personal needs at various bases and hospitals. By 1968, the peak of Red Cross involvement, there were 480 field directors and hospital and recreation workers serving throughout Southeast Asia. In all, Red Cross workers provided nearly two million services to U.S. military personnel caught up in the war. Five of those workers gave their lives, and many others were injured. There were also male nurses and sanitarians sponsored by the Red Cross to work with the refugees in cooperation with the South Vietnam Red Cross and the U.S. Agency for International Development.

"Uncle Jack" lands at a helicopter pad in Vietnam with a morale-boosting passenger wearing a helmet and flak jacket. The young recreation workers were signed up for twelve months of grueling and dangerous duty that included a strict code of ethics. Infractions could send them home faster than outbound mail. Yet, like the wars before it, the Vietnam conflict stirred up occasional rumors of alleged immorality, reflecting the need of a few troops to blame somebody for their plight. As one Red Cross administrator put it, "Perhaps we served as a useful safety valve."

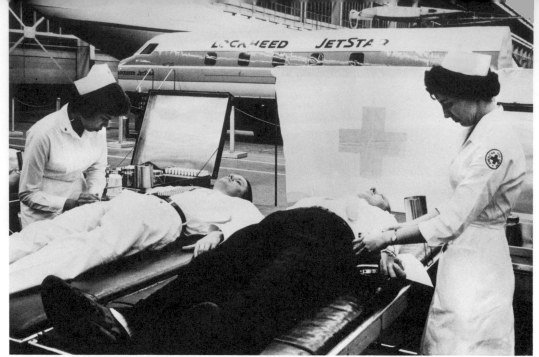

Donors give blood at the Lockheed aircraft plant in Marietta, Georgia. Organized blood drives at factories and office buildings throughout the country continued to be a tremendous source of blood for the Red Cross.

The Red Cross asks the American people to care in 1968.

You can't be there to help them. We can.

Put your money where your boys are.

help
us
help

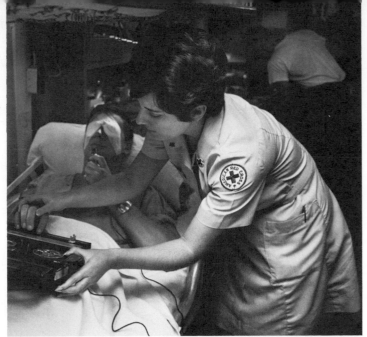

Aboard the hospital ship Sanctuary *off Vietnam, a worker helps a wounded sailor make a recording to send home.*

A New York Red Cross technologist checks blood types while another records them. "Reading" a blood type is a matter of observing whether cells clump together when blood grouping serum is added.

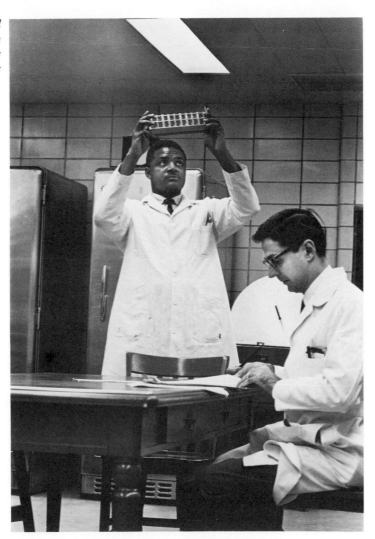

7. Threshold
to a Second Century

The seventies propel the American Red Cross into the electronics age while bringing it to a new awareness of its most vital resource—the volunteer. The organization stands on the threshold of its second century of service besieged by inflation and by fierce competition for available funds and volunteers. It turns to "creative voluntarism," advanced technology and a critical review of its services in an effort to enhance its value to the American public.

Rapid social change and new technology marked the 1970s. The decade also saw the end of the Vietnam War with its nightly televised tales of brutality and death, but not the human problems it left behind. The Red Cross entered the period determined to demonstrate to the country that although it was an organization that worked closely with the military and elsewhere "made things happen," it retained its basic humanitarian motives and humanness. The years found the organization getting deeply involved in activities aimed at helping Americans better their lives through self-help. The Red Cross became more of an advocate for the common good, bringing about needed changes in disaster laws, making volunteers available for federal social projects and influencing the medical field through its rapidly expanding blood research and program activities. But its success depended on the volunteers who offered the country the greatest gift—the gift of self, in terms of both service and donated blood.

It was also a time of introspection for the Red Cross in both the national and chapter sectors that sometimes led to painful change and sacrifice, but more often resulted in self-renewal and pride in meeting America's true needs. The importance of the process was brought home forcefully in 1973, and even more so in 1976, when a Harris poll revealed that few Americans understood the many vital roles that the organization played in their everyday lives. As the organization approached its 1981 centenary, it took up the slogan: "Red Cross: Ready for a New Century," and strove to continue the providing of meaningful service while better educating the public in regard to what was being accomplished.

Modernization went hand and hand with the spirit of renewal, affecting the delivery of services. Men and women in uniform could find ready assistance when trouble struck. The same held true for disaster victims, but the service was quicker and more efficient. The Red Cross had entered the electronics age. Among the tools helping the Red Cross to do its job better were a communications satellite that had a successful debut in 1977 during flooding at Johnstown, Pennsylvania, a sophis-

214

ticated data-processing center, and a thriving in-house production center that turned out audiovisual materials for internal and external use.

The data-processing center revolutionized Red Cross administrative functions. It could compute and store enormous amounts of internal information in a fraction of the time it once took, making the organization more cost efficient. But even more important, it had the potential to save lives. Fifty-seven regional blood centers and twenty subcenters across the country counted on it. As the world's largest collector, processor and distributor of blood and blood derivatives, the Red Cross had a responsibility to provide only the safest products to the nation's hospitals. Blood centers needed merely to dial a Washington number to receive daily lists of names that would allow them effectively to screen out donors suspected of carrying highly transmittable and sometimes fatal hepatitis. As the decade waned, the organization planned for greater utilization of the data center, particularly in the disaster and safety areas.

Innovation and change swept the Red Cross. To keep pace, the organization established an audio-visual production center at Bailey's Crossroads, Virginia, in 1975. The center gave the organization a tool through which it could effectively communicate needed information. Its greatest value lay in the training area. Blood Services could train staff in regional centers in the use of a new processor. The national insurance office could help staff members understand benefits due them under Red Cross life and major medical policies. Community Services could educate both an in-house audience and the public in safety and lifesaving techniques. Long-range plans envisioned even greater utilization to realize the full potential of the center, including a hook-up with an orbiting satellite.

The world of the seventies challenged the Red Cross at the policy level as a more complicated society demanded that the more than 3,100 chapters cope with community problems that did not fall strictly into the emergency category. As in the thirties, chapters had to deal with each situation on an individual basis, concentrating on need rather than circumstances, sometimes risking public censure in the process. Every community had its particular brand of problems and needs. To be labeled relevant required that chapters focus their energies on new services as well as the more traditional. Many worked closely with returning veterans, helping them to adjust to civilian life. Some opened storefront centers in ghetto areas to be nearer their residents. Others vastly expanded their work with forgotten segments of society, including the jailed and the mentally ill. Working closely with the government, chapters also alerted thousands of the elderly and others through federal programs aimed at making sure eligible citizens knew about available benefits such as food stamps or increased monthly social security payments.

The nature of disasters changed too. Natural ones still occurred, requiring costly Red Cross involvement, but manmade ones were growing in profusion. Chemical plant accidents, oil spills and dam breaks were typical of the disasters that kept volunteers and staff busy. By the latter part of the decade, the government had become the primary resource for victims seeking long-term rehabilitation while the Red Cross continued to provide the swift emergency assistance upon which its reputation rested. The nuclear age fully descended in 1979 when the White House summoned Red Cross disaster specialists and told them to begin planning the possible mass evacuation of residents from Three Mile Island, Pennsylvania, site of the nation's first nuclear power plant accident.

Then there were the refugees. Tens of thousands of them fled Indochina following the end of the war in 1975, posing new problems for America and the Red Cross. Chapter volunteers and staff helped at refugee camps on Guam and in the United States and assisted with the later resettlement of more than 100,000 of them in communities across the country. But the mid decade was only the beginning. "Boat people" from Vietnam began arriving in droves in 1979 at camps in Malaysia and elsewhere, seeking assistance and refuge. The American Red Cross joined with other agencies to provide aid, and then in the same year recruited doctors and nurses for service in Thailand, where starving Cambodians sought refuge after fleeing their Communist-dominated homeland.

Throughout the years, the mission of the American Red Cross had been to help people help themselves. The way the Red Cross helped changed dramatically during the seventies. But one thing did not change. The Red Cross still relied on its volunteers to get the job done. Providing the leadership for the millions doing the job over the decade were three volunteer leaders whose appointments by American Presidents to the position of principal officer of the organization transcended political boundaries and highlighted the impartiality of the Red Cross. They were E. Roland Harriman, who during his twenty-three years served under appointments from Presidents Harry S. Truman, Dwight D. Eisenhower, John F. Kennedy, Lyndon B. Johnson and Richard M. Nixon; Frank Stanton, former president of the Columbia Broadcasting System, initially appointed by Nixon in 1973 and later reappointed by President Gerald R. Ford; and Dr. Jerome H. Holland, former ambassador to Sweden and former president of Hampton Institute in Virginia, who was appointed by President Jimmy Carter in 1979. They had different backgrounds but a common quest—"one Red Cross" unity, greater and more meaningful volunteer involvement, and service excellence. Through their leadership and the work of the many volunteers, the Red Cross stood ready to enter its second century of service in 1981 as an organization built upon the indomitable spirit of the American people who made its existence possible and its future mission necessary.

Throughout the decade, despite a lengthy interlude of peace, Red Cross expenses for services to the military, to veterans and to their families consistently remained close to the $50 million mark, far outdistancing all other services except blood. One fifth of the organization's budget went for fulfillment of this charter obligation, yet in 1976, only 19 percent of the American people realized that the Red Cross provided such services. During the Vietnam War, most people knew.

Lieutenant Colonel J. L. Hughes, a downed U.S. Air Force pilot with head wounds, walks barefoot between two guards in North Vietnam in 1969. The American Red Cross rallied public support against the "inhumane treatment" of the prisoners, who were considered war criminals without rights by the Vietnamese Communists. In 1970, Hanoi allowed the organization to send bimonthly food packages to the 1,137 U.S. prisoners.

"Protest!" The American Red Cross urges citizens to write directly to Hanoi, demanding the end of alleged "inhumane POW treatment." The North Vietnamese refused to allow inspections of detention camps in 1971, claiming that downed U.S. pilots and others were "war criminals" and therefore not eligible for protection under the Geneva Convention. The American Red Cross had launched its massive "Write Hanoi!" campaign in October 1969, hoping to soften the Communist stand by weighing public opinion against them.

217

A bank of high-speed telecommunications machines at national headquarters brings in word from American Red Cross offices around the world, the bulk of it on behalf of military personnel overseas. In 1979, nearly 634,000 welfare and emergency messages were relayed to and from the chapters who serviced them every 49.75 seconds.

A field director in Vietnam shares a joke with two soldiers while carrying his work into a front-line area during the war. Red Cross personnel often worked long hours under hardship conditions in an effort to help servicemen resolve personal problems or to help them get home when emergency leave was granted because of death or serious illness in the immediate family.

In the early morning hours, two recreation workers somberly await a helicopter that will take them to an outlying fire base. In Vietnam, a short helicopter ride could bring rear-echelon people face to face with death.

Christmas Day at a fire base in Vietnam. GI's open Red Cross "ditty bags" containing comfort items. Chapter volunteers and Youth Services members put together nearly three million of them for the troops during the Vietnam War.

Throughout the war, military commanders called the services of the Red Cross "indispensable" and "prime factors" in their efforts to sustain the morale of the troops. The dedicated service also pointed up the difference of viewpoint existing between other national societies and the American Red Cross. The American Red Cross was bound by its charter to provide welfare services to the ablebodied troops on duty, an obligation some societies felt violated the neutrality principle of the International Red Cross.

"Are you sure you're not peeking?" A recreation worker checks a GI's blindfold at Fire Base Jamie in Vietnam. The fire base was one of several front-line areas visited regularly by American Red Cross girls attempting to keep up the often flagging morale through games and other organized activities.

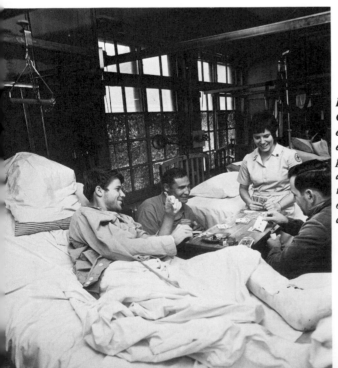

Diversionary recreation. A card game helps patients at the base hospital at Camp Zama, Japan, pass the time. Therapeutic recreation, on the other hand, embraced a wider range of activities, such as handicrafts, which required the expertise of especially trained Red Cross personnel, as it was geared to a patient's individual rehabilitation needs. In 1976, the recreation program was drastically cut back in a cost-reduction action that removed professional recreation personnel from the military hospitals, despite protests from commanding officers. By 1979, it was apparent that the use of volunteers alone was insufficient to keep recreation programs alive and they had all but disappeared.

With the end of the Vietnam War, the American Red Cross phased out its Supplemental Recreational Activities Overseas program with the able-bodied troops, and eventually withdrew its professional personnel from recreation programs in military hospitals.

At the height of the Vietnam War, a volunteer for Service to Military Families meets the wife of a serviceman at the Atlanta airport to help her cope with a personal crisis.

A disabled veteran discusses a problem with a Service to Veterans worker at the Atlanta, Georgia, chapter in 1970. The veteran had returned to college despite one amputated leg and another that was partially paralyzed. Volunteers and staff concentrated on helping veterans readjust to civilian life, and that often meant assisting them with paperwork connected with their benefits.

Mass exoduses of Indochinese became commonplace during the middle to late 1970s. The American Red Cross became involved in a major one in the spring of 1975. As the governments of South Vietnam and Cambodia threatened to collapse, the American Red Cross helped with "Operation Baby Lift," which brought some two thousand infants and toddlers to the United States for adoption. Following the fall of the South Vietnamese and Cambodian governments, the organization set to work on Operation New Life, which officially began on April 23, 1975. Refugees fleeing their homelands were brought to various points in the Pacific for eventual resettlement in the United States and elsewhere, and thousands of volunteers and staff on both sides of the Pacific helped make the transition a little easier.

Old army barracks at Fort Chaffee, Arkansas, which became home to thousands of refugees from Indochina. More than 130,000 of them took up new lives in America following their processing through Chaffee and camps at Eglin Air Force Base, Florida; Camp Pendleton, California, and Fort Indiantown Gap, Pennsylvania, where the Red Cross teamed up with government authorities and other voluntary agencies to provide a multitude of services. The Refugee Locator Service set up at national headquarters was still operating in 1979, when a new exodus of Indochinese refugees began arriving, bringing about expansion of that service. And at the chapter level, volunteers made the adjustment to a new culture a little easier in 1975 by teaching the refugees English, providing transportation, ironing out problems with government benefit programs, giving emergency assistance, and by just letting the refugees know that help was available.

Senator Edward Kennedy of Massachusetts, chairman of the Senate's subcommittee on refugees, speaks to newsmen at Dulles Airport in Washington in August 1978, following the successful culmination of efforts to have Communist Vietnam allow Vietnamese citizens with American passports to leave. Joining Kennedy in meeting the first group of refugees is Red Cross President George M. Elsey (right). The American Red Cross worked closely with the International Red Cross and the Senate subcommittee to bring about the refugees' freedom to travel. Many of the Vietnamese were married to American citizens, including former servicemen.

Starvation in Cambodia in 1979 brought in medical teams from Red Cross societies around the world, including the American Red Cross. Nurses and doctors across the United States responded to the call for help. They were screened by the American Red Cross, inoculated against a host of diseases ranging from leprosy to typhoid fever, and flown to refugee camps in Thailand, where tens of thousands of Cambodians lay suffering. In December 1979, the situation eased somewhat as the Cambodian government decided to allow the Red Cross and UNICEF to fly supplies into the interior of Cambodia, removing a major obstacle to getting adequate food supplies to the starving.

A Loretto nursing sister from America draws a curious crowd at the Kamput refugee camp in Thailand, where she puts her pediatrics skills to work for starving Cambodians through the International Committee of the Red Cross. There were 2,200 refugees at the mountain camp in December 1979, mainly young people between fifteen and twenty-five who had lost their families during fighting in Kampuchea [Cambodia].

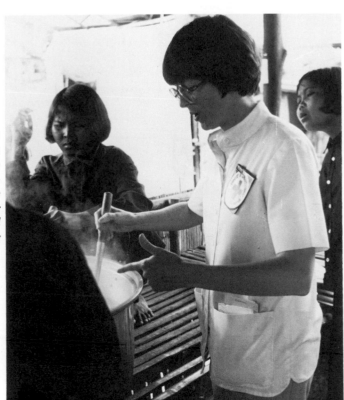

Natural disasters granted no stays during the 1970s. The decade had its share of flooding and hurricanes.

People in need remained the focus of attention for the Red Cross in the 1970s. There was no shortage of crises or human needs, but there was sometimes criticism when Red Cross volunteers helped run strike-bound hospitals, provided food and shelter to Indians warring with government agencies, or assisted striking workers with necessities. "The mission of the Red Cross," said new president George Elsey in October 1970, "requires adherence to an inviolable principle that its services and programs be made available to all solely on the basis of need and without regard to race, color, religion, sex, or national origin."

A photographer brings a grin to the face of a disaster victim at Frankfort, Kentucky, following his visit to a clothing truck run by the Seventh-Day Adventists, one of the religious groups with which the American Red Cross works closely when trouble strikes.

Dr. Jerome H. ("Brud") Holland (right) is introduced to a volunteer by a chapter worker following tornado devastation in April 1979 at Wichita Falls, Texas. It was Holland's first official inspection trip as newly appointed chairman of the American Red Cross. A major concern facing the chairman was the need for additional disaster funds at a time when the national economy was experiencing a slowdown. The year ending June 30, 1979, saw the Red Cross spend $36.6 million on disaster relief during operations in forty-nine states, Puerto Rico, the Virgin Islands and the Mariana Islands.

An emergency van for the American Red Cross races down a road at Three Mile Island, Pennsylvania, in 1979 while the nation awaits official reaction to the first nuclear power plant accident. At issue was whether the leak of radioactive materials at the plant (background) was enough to warrant the evacuation of the area's residents. Some two thousand Red Cross volunteers helped chapters in nearby counties plan for the possible evacuation of 300,000 persons who would have to be housed and fed for a considerable time. Fortunately, the danger was reported as minimal and a relatively small number of persons actually sought Red Cross assistance.

Seventy-two licensed nuclear power plants around the country in 1979 posed a new threat to Americans—radioactive dangers through equipment breakdowns. The Red Cross readied itself for possible mass evacuations of citizens from endangered areas.

Disaster assistance took on a space age look in the summer of 1977. The Red Cross and the Communications Satellite Corporation successfully tested an experimental system for disaster communications when flooding swept the Johnstown, Pennsylvania, area July 20, killing and injuring nearly three thousand persons and making thousands of others homeless. Volunteers maintained a link with outside radio operators via satellite, making it possible to process some seventeen thousand welfare inquiries from concerned friends and relatives despite the breakdown in normal communications.

A disaster drill finds a Red Cross worker manning equipment for tracking and operating a satellite jointly launched by the Comsat Corporation and the American Red Cross to improve the latter's communications system in emergencies. The satellite also helped meet the organization's internal communications needs.

Red Cross volunteers take to snowmobiles to deliver relief supplies to Buffalo, New York, residents stranded in their homes in February 1977 by extreme cold and mountainous snowdrifts. Chapters from Illinois to New Jersey provided services to people stranded or affected by fuel shortages.

Cooperation between the Red Cross and the federal government was highlighted during the winter of 1978 when sixty thousand pounds of foodstuffs were airlifted to Cincinnati following appeals by disaster workers there. Within hours, donated food from the Department of Agriculture was being distributed by volunteers from the Red Cross and other agencies in snow-bound Ohio, Kentucky and Indiana.

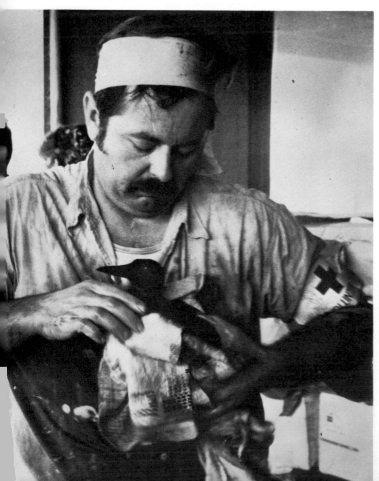

Sign of the times. A San Francisco volunteer cleans oil off the feathers of a seagull that was exposed to an oil slick in February 1971, following a collision between two tankers. The accident caused 840,000 gallons of oil to spill into San Francisco Bay and posed an immediate threat to wildlife. The Red Cross set up a bird-cleaning station and a first-aid and feeding station for the many concerned people who showed up to help.

Disaster relief evolved into a highly disciplined science during the seventies, but the basic philosophy laid down by Barton and Bicknell remained unchanged: Send appropriate supplies. Work closely with government and community agencies. Provide mass care as needed. Treat families as whole units, basing assistance on needs, not losses. Make all disaster aid an outright gift.

People were sometimes their own worst enemies, responsible for oil spills, hostage taking and fires.

The kiss of life. A fireman gives artificial respiration to a child overcome by smoke.

Victims of a siege on several buildings in Washington, D.C., by a radical group in March 1977 are driven away from the scene in a Red Cross vehicle. The Hanafi Muslim group killed one person, wounded several and took 149 hostages. The incident lasted two days, and involved over 150 volunteers from the District of Columbia and other metropolitan area chapters. They worked around the clock from eight fixed and mobile sites, providing first aid, food, comfort articles and transportation for hostages and police.

A Red Cross disaster volunteer comforts a child following a tenement fire in New York City in 1972.

Having lost her possessions, the future looking bleak, an elderly victim of a fire in San Francisco seeks solace.

A St. Louis, Missouri, fireman enjoys a hot cup of coffee while battling a blaze at an apartment house in the winter of 1977. Red Cross vans and volunteers are a steady source of assistance to fire departments, which have little time to attend to the comforts and needs of the victims or themselves. Chapters, regardless of size, must meet the needs of disaster victims to the best of their ability or risk violating the organization's congressional charter.

A weary and bewildered youngster eats in a disaster shelter at Man, West Virginia, following heavy flooding in February 1972.

No rummage sale. A disaster worker interviews a woman at Calion, Arkansas, who suffered heavy losses when tornadoes and floods combined to bring havoc to the state in June 1974. Disaster assistance may include food, clothing, temporary rent payments, home furnishings, medical care, eyeglass replacement, building repair supplies, occupational tools, and other items essential to a family's recovery.

Hurricane Agnes roared into the East in June 1972 to distinguish itself as one of the worst disasters of the decade, testing the mettle of nearly 29,000 Red Cross volunteers and some 1,300 staff. Government rehabilitation loans to victims in twelve states spared the Red Cross multi-million-dollar expenses that would have overwhelmed its resources, but the operation still cost the organization a staggering $23 million. The statistics spoke for themselves: 668 Red Cross shelters opened, 178,312 people sheltered, 527,863 people fed and given first aid or other forms of mass care. The operation went on into late summer, exhausting Red Cross disaster funds.

Hurricane Agnes displays her force in a satellite photograph taken in June 1972.

Flood victims are carried to safety by Red Cross volunteers helping to evacuate the B'nai B'rith home in Wilkes-Barre, Pennsylvania, in the summer of 1972. The waters of the Susquehanna River had inundated large sections of the state.

A military helicopter delivers relief supplies for the Red Cross at Wilkes-Barre, Pennsylvania.

A Red Cross poster tells citizens at Harrisburg, Pennsylvania, that free assistance to meet their needs is available. The storm caused $1.7 billion in damages, killed 122 people and left nearly 12,-000 injured or ill. Central Pennsylvania and southern New York bore the brunt of the flooding that followed the onslaught of the hurricane. In Wilkes-Barre, Pennsylvania, and Corning, New York, the housing shortage was so great that Red Cross shelters had to stay open for two months after the initial flooding.

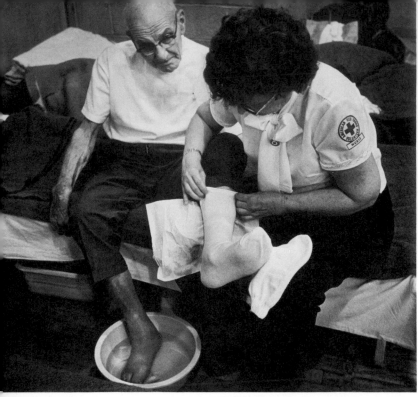

A nursing home patient evacuated during Hurricane Agnes has his feet bathed at a disaster shelter.

"The Red Cross got here right after the flood hit us, and I never saw people work so hard in all my life. They did everything to try to make us comfortable. They gave us food. They brought in blankets and mattresses. They nursed the sick. Until then I didn't realize how much the Red Cross could mean to us!"

Pennsylvania disaster victim
Hurricane Agnes, 1972

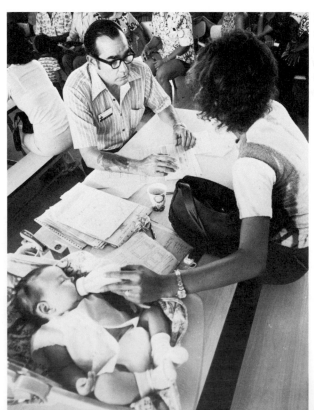

Typhoon Pamela sweeps Guam in May 1976, sending victims rushing to Red Cross shelters for assistance. This mother, trying to feed her baby while answering questions about her family's needs, represented just one of the 23,000 families requiring assistance.

Local merchants in Agana, Guam, vie for Red Cross vouchers given free to victims of the May 1976 typhoon who need clothing.

After nearly 100 years, the Red Cross of the 1970s continued to be dependent on America's generosity. By 1979, more than half of the 3,108 chapters were in United Way partnerships, a trend that began in the early 1950s. The rest relied on independent annual campaigns for members and funds, usually in March Red Cross Month. Moneys also came in from disaster fund raising, federal research grants, hospital fees for the processing of blood products, Youth Services enrollment fees, special events, deferred gifts such as bequests, foundation grants and interest on endowment and securities funds. Although some favored it, the Red Cross received no appropriated funding from the government, allowing it to preserve its freedom of action on behalf of the American people. Logistical support by the government for the organization's work during disasters and in connection with its work with the military continued to be the only federal aid given.

A fund-raising poster encourages giving to the Red Cross through the United Way. Federated fund raising was an easier way for chapters to raise money, but it had a disadvantage. There was a danger of complacency that could affect their ability to raise sufficient funds to meet their own program requirements as well as their obligatory support of national services. It therefore became imperative that chapters recruit knowledgeable volunteers to represent Red Cross interests during negotiations with local United Way boards, who determined agency allocations. It was also important that the chapters actively help the United Way's campaign for funds. A major policy statement was issued in December 1979 which reiterated that each "chapter must retain exclusively the determination and control of the composition of its own budget and the amount it shall ask from the public during the annual fund raising campaign." Chapters also were expected to hold fund drives to meet emergencies such as wars or disasters. Additionally, the chapters were instructed to reject any United Way moneys if restrictions were imposed that prevented them from supporting the national sector with its charter obligations of serving the military and coping with America's disasters.

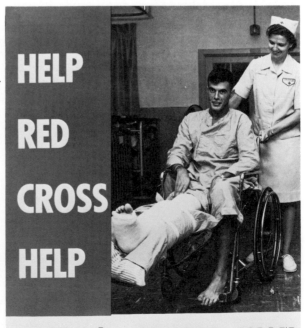

HELP RED CROSS HELP

...the UNITED WAY

The Accounting and Auditing Office of American Red Cross headquarters streamlines its operation through computer technology. The organization is audited annually by the Department of Defense and the findings forwarded to the U.S. Congress in accordance with its federal charter. In 1979, the annual report revealed that the Red Cross spent $375,599,354 in providing services to the American people. Of that amount, only 8.5 percent was spent on fund raising and general management functions, far below many other charitable organizations.

An in-house audiovisual studio provided Red Cross headquarters with a new way of communicating with chapter workers, field staff and the public.

Chairman Frank Stanton prepares for a 1978 appearance in a segment of the Red Cross Contact *series, a videotape project aimed at developing better communications between management and volunteers and staff in the field. It kept the field abreast of policy developments, new services offered by chapters, and the operational role of the Red Cross in major disasters and other newsworthy events over the months.*

President George M. Elsey and chairman Frank Stanton are the focal point for cameras at the Red Cross audiovisual production center at Bailey's Crossroads, Virginia. The center, which officially bears Stanton's name, produced an average of seventy productions yearly between 1975, the year of its establishment, and 1979. These mainly included videotape cassettes and films of an instructional nature and public service radio and television spots.

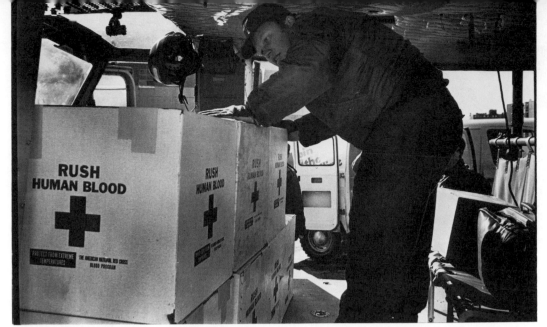

A helicopter crewman prepares to deliver blood for the American Red Cross at Boston following blizzards which swept the East Coast in February 1978 shutting down traffic and preventing the functioning of essential services.

Blood Services grew sophisticated during the decade. New medical technology enabled the fifty-seven regional centers and twenty subcenters to turn their attention from whole blood and plasma to blood derivatives and research into a host of hereditary diseases. New techniques also made it possible for the Red Cross to utilize collected blood to its fullest, making nearly every drop of it count. Nearly four million American donors in 1979 helped the organization to remain the world's largest collector, processor and distributor of donated blood and blood products.

A pheresis donor relaxes while a special instrument separates plasma platelets or white cells and returns the red blood cells. The whole procedure took from two to three hours and was said to be painless. Despite the drain on a donor's time, volunteer donations increased yearly. People undergoing cancer therapy and those with leukemia or aplastic anemia were sometimes dependent on the procedure, which made white cells or platelets (small cells that induce clotting) available for transfusion.

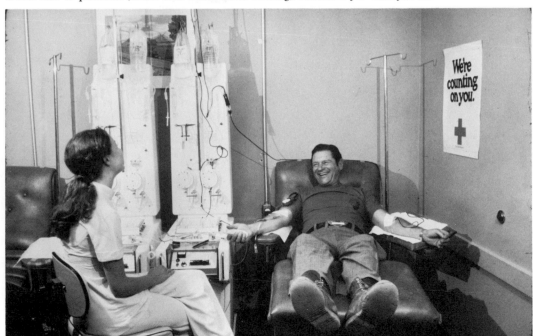

A reference technologist for the Red Cross conducts a test in typing and cross matching of red blood cells as part of an ongoing service to hospitals served by the Tidewater Regional Blood Services in Norfolk, Virginia.

The American Red Cross Blood Services collected more than half of the nation's total blood donations in the 1970s and took those only from voluntary donors. The Red Cross insistence on voluntary donations stemmed from ethical considerations, as well as from awareness of the higher incidence of hepatitis among paid donors.

After thirty-one years, the American Red Cross Blood Services achieved a monthly record in March 1979, collecting over 480,000 units of blood. It was a fitting ending for the presidentially proclaimed annual Red Cross Month.

A life is saved in 1967. J. D. Thompson, an electric lineman with Red Cross certification in first aid, gives artificial respiration to a fellow worker knocked unconscious by 2,400 volts of electricity atop a power pole in Jacksonville, Florida. The man began breathing shortly after and regained consciousness. Thompson received the organization's Extraordinary Personal Action award for his efforts.

"When a life is saved by a Red Cross trained person, the great value of first aid, small craft, and water safety training is dramatically demonstrated," stated an official Red Cross brochure in 1978. To recognize lifesaving acts, the Red Cross made awards, the highest being the Certificate of Merit. It was awarded for any act adjudged meritorious in saving or sustaining a life, and carried the signatures of the President of the United States and the chairman of the American Red Cross. The Certificate of Merit was given only to persons who had taken a Red Cross course. Others received a Certificate of Recognition if Red Cross skills were used. The Certificate of Merit was established in 1928 and more than six thousand certificates have been issued since then.

A Cardio Pulmonary Resuscitation (CPR) course under way at a Red Cross chapter. Students use a rubber manikin named "Resusci Annie" to avoid accidents that might occur during practice if external heart compression were allowed on live subjects. CPR was considered the most effective way to revive persons whose breathing had stopped but much more complicated than mouth-to-mouth resuscitation. The Red Cross worked closely with the American Heart Association during the mid 1970s to teach the new method.

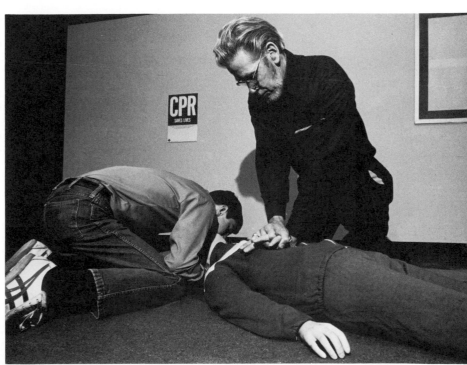

Most swimming facilities are guarded by lifeguards holding Red Cross certification. In 1979, the chapters certified nearly 2.3 million persons who had reached certain levels of water safety skills as a result of Red Cross training, and sent another 180,000 out to teach others.

237

Preschool children learn to respect the water without fear during a Red Cross swimming class at a YMCA in Dayton, Ohio. Emphasis is on a one-child-one-adult ratio to make the lessons effective. Since the start of the water safety program in 1914, the Red Cross has worked closely with the YMCA. The "Y" often provides the pool, the Red Cross the instructors.

Carried on mainly by volunteers, first-aid and water safety instruction continued to be vital community programs. The greatest thrill for an instructor was to have a former student cited for saving a life.

A handicapped child responds joyously to the feeling of freedom that she experiences in a pool with her volunteer Red Cross instructor for Adapted Aquatics. All instruction is based on the disabled person's individual capabilities, a method which allows chapter instructors to work with a wide range of students suffering from physiological and mental impairments. In addition to safety reasons, the goal is to give the students a sense of accomplishment, increased strength and a social opportunity to be with others.

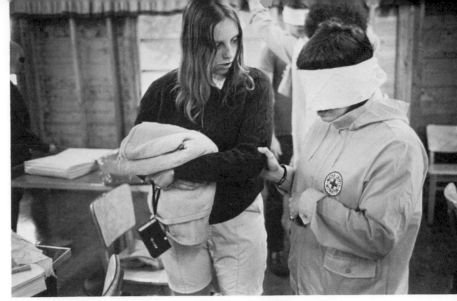

To effectively teach the blind to swim, one should know what it feels like to be blind. Students at an aquatic school at Honesdale, Pennsylvania, in 1971 simulate the problems of a blind student as they seek certification as chapter instructors in Adapted Aquatics for the handicapped.

A chapter volunteer helping out at the state fair in Gaithersburg, Maryland, in August 1978 is caught in an off-guard moment. Seventy-four volunteers helped dispense 21,000 glasses of water from a disaster van to crowds attending the week-long fair.

The year 1970 saw the American Red Cross give special attention to the elderly. This volunteer reads to a man in a nursing home.

A royal visitor to Red Cross national headquarters. Mrs. Cynthia Wedel, national chairman of volunteers, escorts Japanese Princess Hitachi (left) into the headquarters, April 5, 1978. Wedel, also the first woman to be elected president of the National Council of Churches, led the volunteers for six years, turning over her duties to Mrs. Joan Knox in 1979.

A chapter volunteer helps a handicapped girl from the back of a chapter car after driving her to a therapy session. Nearly 1.4 million volunteers served in 1979, performing a myriad of jobs, from providing meals-on-wheels for the elderly to running nurseries in courthouses where parents were involved in cases. The Red Cross tries to avoid duplicating the services of other agencies, and when its expertise is no longer required, turns over to community groups many of the services that it originally started.

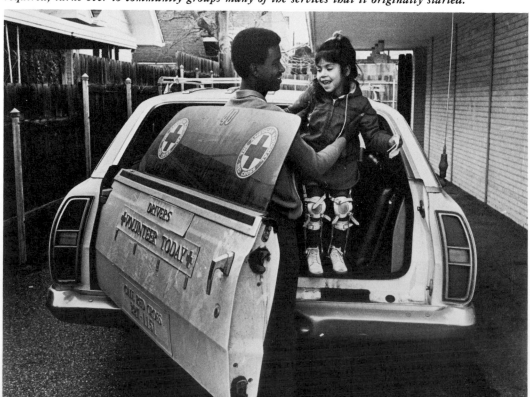

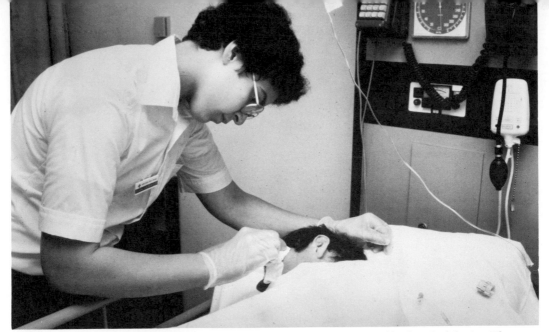

A Red Cross Youth Service volunteer attends to a cardiac patient as part of his hospital duties. The 1970s found chapters involving youth in more meaningful activities than had been the pattern in the past, particularly at the high school level. Young people represented youth interests on chapter boards and participated as blood donors. They carried out home repairs for the elderly and the poor. They taught first-aid, water-safety and home-nursing courses and they launched New Pride, a service in some chapters that was designed to encourage juvenile offenders to become their best possible selves through self-improvement activities, job training and assistance in finding part-time work. They also engaged in "peer counseling," particularly in such areas as alcoholism and venereal diseases.

A woman inmate at the county jail in Houston, Texas, sews a Red Cross patch on a smock for volunteers. Recognizing the need to involve all segments of society, many chapters around the country in 1971 were finding volunteers in places such as prisons. Although behind bars, the inmates sewed useful articles—"ditty bags" for servicemen overseas, quilts for disaster victims, and aprons for nurses, health aides, and others.

Prologue to a New Century

"What is past is prologue," wrote Shakespeare in Act II of *The Tempest.* I agree; my firmest prejudice is that history is the most valuable single asset in preparing for the future. From this pictorial history of the American Red Cross we are reminded of the many sources of our present strength, but we are also made aware of past weaknesses that blemish the record.

We have a clear perception of the varying ways in which our predecessors met the social and economic challenges of their times. We see that change has been the one constant in the services American have provided their fellow Americans through the Red Cross. Lithographs, woodcuts, photographs and even cartoons carry us through one hundred years, from the time when the Red Cross was little more than one dedicated woman, to the present, when millions of Red Cross volunteers mirror the United States as it is today. The lesson is clear: The one imperative for this organization is that there be constant evolution of its services and that those services meet America's needs through Americans themselves.

Millions of volunteers and professional staff served through the American Red Cross during the first hundred years, but a few deserve special credit for accelerating that evolutionary process. Clara Barton's foresight made a European idea better by turning the Red Cross into a practical force. And yet it took Mabel Boardman to turn the Red Cross into a stable organization that offered a broad array of services through chapters chartered by a national headquarters, and that carried out its mandates through well-trained volunteers supported by competent professional staff.

One of the supervolunteers remaining after World War II, E. Roland Harriman, would lead the Red Cross to modernization in 1947 by bringing about critically important changes in the 1905 charter, which included the replacement of the self-perpetuating Central Committee with a broadly based, democratically elected Board of Governors. It is impossible to overstate the significance of this change, which granted chapters considerable control over the direction of the national organization. Services, finances, structure, relationships with government and other organizations —all these would be determined by volunteers tuned in to the social needs of the nation. Their ready acceptance of the challenges confronting a fast-changing society brought about the explosion of social services in the 1950s, '60s and '70s, so well portrayed in these pages.

On coming to the closing chapter, the question arises: "What will the 1980s and later decades mean to the Red Cross?" I would rather phrase the question: "What will the Red Cross mean to the nation in the '80s and beyond?"

242

In the early days of the Red Cross, our forebears faced the reality of a suddenly closed frontier. The days of expansion to seemingly limitless new farmlands were gone forever. Red Crossers helped the nation transform itself into an urban industrial society from a largely rural, largely agricultural land. Now, at the onset of our second century, we face for the first time in our national history shortages of energy and natural resources. The days of economic growth without limit seem to be over. American society will be transformed in ways we do not yet perceive clearly.

America need not fear the future, nor should the Red Cross. If Shakespeare is right, then we can have confidence. In its first century, the American Red Cross has evolved into a great national tradition of voluntary service. Millions of men, women and youth have educated people to help themselves and to help each other. Voluntary service will continue, but as the nation confronts future challenges, it will take new forms. Red Cross service rests on the bedrock philosophy that Americans can make the country a better place to live in by working together through voluntarism. We cannot predict the future, but we are ready to stake our destiny on the indomitable spirit of the American people, who have made America the greatest of countries.

And so we lay this volume down, not with nostalgia for the past, but with conviction that the lessons of its first hundred years will provide a secure foundation for the Red Cross to meet the challenges of the future through new services, new relationships and new talents.

George M. Elsey, President
American Red Cross

Index

Numbers in *italic* refer to illustrations; *plates* refer to color illustrations following page 86.

Allenby, Field Marshal Lord, 52
ambulance services: American
　Ambulance group, *12*
　World War I and postwar, 65,
　74, *74, 75, 128*
American Ambulance group, *12*
American Association for the Re-
　lief of Misery on the Batt-
　lefield, 12
American Association of the Red
　Cross, *see* American Red
　Cross
American First Aid Association, 3
American Heart Association, 237
The American Magazine, 29
American National Red Cross, *see*
　American Red Cross
American Red Cross: Board of
　Governors, 173, 174, 176,
　182, 243
　Central Committee, 34, 55,
　108, 112, 137, 172, 176,
　243
　chapters, 66, 104, 111, 115,
　173, 174, 176, 215, 233; au-
　tonomous, 2, 13, 14, 29;
　under national headquarters,
　32, 34, 243; *see also* finances;
　racism; volunteers *below*
　charter, 217, 220, 233; (1900),
　2, 4, 29; after reorganization
　(1905), 32, 33, 34, 53;
　amended (1947), 173, 176,
　176, 243
　communications and media,
　109, 129, 199, 214–15, *218,*
　218, 225, 225, 234, 234; see
　also *American Red Cross Bulle-*
　tin; Red Cross Courier; Red
　Cross Magazine
　conventions and meetings:
　(1916), *52;* (1921), 52;
　(1929), 120; (1938), 115;
　(1947), 173, 176; (1964),
　208
　criticisms of personnel and
　policies, 21, 22, 55, 111,
　113, 114, 159, 181, 211; *see*
　also racism *below*
　Executive Committee, 2, 3, 53,
　97
　emblem, flag, and name, 2
　finances (funding; member-
　ship): accountable to Con-
　gress, 32, 35, 234, *234;* ce-
　lebrities, *108, 121, 129;* early
　years, 2, 14, 15, 16, *17,* 22,
　28; foundations, 52, 59,
　67; government funding re-
　fused, 95, 111, 112, 113,
　233; institutional member-
　ship, 49; 1920s and 1930s,
　104, 108, *120, 121;* 1950s to
　present, 173, 176, *177,* 203,

ARC, finances *(cont'd)*
　214, 215, *224,* 230, 233,
　233, 234; after reorganiza-
　tion, 32, 33, *43;* and united
　community drives, 120, 173,
　215, 233, *233;* World War I
　and postwar, 55, 56, 58, 60,
　61, *61,* 62, 64, 70, *70,* 71,
　82, 95; World War II and
　postwar, 137, *141,* 142, 143,
　145, 151, 159; *see also* posters
　formation and founding, 1, 4,
　11, 12, 13, *13,* 15, 243
　headquarters, *31, 34;* perma-
　nent, 32, 51, *51,* 52
　name, changes in, 13
　posters, *see* posters
　racism in personnel and poli-
　cies, *21,* 68, *68,* 69, 104,
　109, 142, 143, 150, *150,*
　151, 153, *153, 156,* 182
　reform and reorganization,
　2–3, 6, 29, *30,* 31, 32
　uniforms and insignia, *83, 115*
　volunteers: early years, ix, *2,*
　16, 21; 1920s and 1930s,
　95–96, 110–11, 114, 115,
　117; 1950s to present, 143,
　173–74, 176, 179, 194,
　194–96, 195, 198, 199, 201,
　203, 205, 214–16, 219, 220,
　221, 222, 224, 225, 226, 228,
　229, 231, 233, 234, 238,
　239–42, 241, 243, 244;
　World War I, 56, 63, 65, 66,
　67, *83;* World War II, 96,
　133, 134, 139, *140,* 141–49,
　144, 146–48, 151, *153,* 154,
　154, 158, 164, *164, 166,*
　168, 168, 171, 172; plate 23;
　see also youth
　War Council, 55, 56, 60, 61,
　64, 67, 88
　Woman's Advisory Commit-
　tee, 55, 67, *67,* 83
　see also United States govern-
　ment
American Red Cross Bulletin, 44,
　72; *plate 2*
American Red Cross Sanitary
　Commission, 59
Anchorage (Alaska), *205*
Andersonville (Ga.), 8, *9*
Andrea Doria, 207, 208
Anthony, Susan B., *20*
Arkansas *Gazette, 105*
Armenia, 2, 17
Armour's calendar, *plate 1*
Arthur, Chester A., 13, 14
Asahi, 102
Ashe, Elizabeth: *Intimate Letters
　from France 1917–19,* 77
Atlanta (Ga.), 135, *194, 221*
Austria, 59, 90, *170, 188,* 189

Baltimore (Md.), *156*
　Institute for the Blind, 93
Barton, Clara (Clarissa) Harlowe,
　1, 3–4, 6, *7,* 20, 31, *31*
　American First Aid Associa-
　tion, 3
　American Red Cross, 1–3, 4,
　11, *13,* 15–23, *18, 19,* 27,
　28, 30, 41, 227, 243; contro-
　versy and resignation, 2–3,
　6, 29, *30,* 31, 32
　Civil War, 1, 4, 5, 6, 8, *8–10,*
　9, 14
　Franco-Prussian War, 10, 11
　Geneva Convention sup-
　ported, 1, 4, 11, 12, *13*
　Russo-Japanese War, *29*
　Spanish-American War, 2, 23,
　23, 25, 25
　writing and lectures, 1, 3, 9,
　10, 11, 14, 15, 20
　Bay of Pigs, *190, 191, 191*
Beale, David: *Through the Johns-
　town Flood,* 22
Beaufort (S.C.), *18*
Bellows, Dr. Henry W., *12*
Bell Telephone Company, 106
Belmont, Eleanor Robson: *The
　Fabric of Memory, 83*
Bergen, Edgar, *129*
Berlin, Irving, *141*
Bicknell, Ernest Percy, 33, 47,
　103, 227
Biloxi (Miss.), *200*
Bissell, Emily P., *43*
blind (assistance and programs),
　93, 115, 194, *194, 239*
blood programs and research,
　133, 134, 173, 177–79, *177–*
　79, 182, 214, 215, 217, 233,
　235, *235, 236, 236,* 241;
　plate 35
　Korean War, 179, 180, *180,*
　182, *182, 184*
　Plasma for Britain, 133, 134,
　135
　segregation policy, 150, 153,
　156, 182
　Vietnam War, *212, 213*
　World War II, 96, 133–35,
　134–36, 142, 144, *145,* 150,
　153, *156–58, 157, 158,* 183;
　plate 31
Boardman, Mabel Thorp, 2, *29,*
　109, *109*
　American Red Cross, 2, 29, 32,
　33, *34,* 35, 38, 39, 42, *42,*
　47, 51, *52,* 55, 58, 66, 67, *67,*
　97, *98,* 107, *109, 109,* 110,
　111, 114, 115, 143, 147,
　172, *172,* 243; Barton at-
　tacked, 2–3, 6, 29, *30,* 31,
　32; *Under the Red Cross Flag,*
　54

Baltimore (Md.)... boating safety, *see* safety
Bonham, Howard, *176*
Borland, William P., 31
Boswell, Connie, *129*
Bowles, Charles S., 5
Boy Scouts, 50, 99
Brady, Mathew B., *4, 7*
Braille Transcription Service, 115
British Isles: World War I, 72, *73,*
　74, 85
　World War II, 132, *132, 133,*
　134, 152, *152, 153,* 159,
　161, *162*
Bromfield, Louis, 75
Buffalo (N.Y.), *226*
Bunker, Ellsworth, 174
Burma, *155*
Butte (Mont.), *83*

Cabinese, Bernard, *176*
Cambodia, *see* Indochinese re-
　fugees
Camp Hoffman (N.C.), *136*
Camp Kilmer (N.J.), *189*
Camp Perry (Fla.), *21*
Camp Sherman (Ohio), 68
Camp Thomas (Ga.), 24
Canal Zone, 34
canteens, clubmobiles, and feed-
　ing vans, *200, 227, 229*
　Korean War, *184, 185*
　World War I, 55, 66, 69, 72,
　72, 73, 87
　World War II, 142, *153,* 155,
　158, *158–60,* 159, 161, *164*
Cherry (Ill.), 38
Chicago Herald, 59
China, 90, 103, *103, 189*
　World War II, *139, 140,* 155,
　155
Christmas Seals, 33, 39, *42–44*
Cincinnati (Ohio), 66, 117
Cincinnati Enquirer, 203
Civil War, 1, 4, *4–6,* 5, 6, 8, 9,
　9, 12, 51
Cleveland Herald, 9
Collins, Gen. James F., 174
Coolidge, Calvin, *107*
Coolidge, Mrs. Calvin, *107*
Council Bluffs (Iowa), *203*
Cowley, Malcolm, 75
Cuba: Bay of Pigs, *190, 191, 191*
　Spanish-American War, 2, 23,
　23–27

Dansville (N.Y.), *14,* 15
Danville (Va.), *154*
Davey, Martin, 124
Davis, Norman H., 139, *141,*
　142, 151, 153, 156, 159
Davis, Richard Harding: *The Red-
　Cross Girl,* 47
Davison, Henry P., 55, 60, 61,
　68, *88,* 97

Day, Richard M., 163
Dayton (Ohio), 48, 49, 238
DeForest, Robert W., 60, 97
Delano, Jane, 21, 33, 45, 58, 77

Denver (Colo.), 148
disaster relief, 1-2, 14-22, 16-22, 32-36, 35-38, 39, 47, 48, 49, 95, 104, 104, 105, 111-13, 112, 113, 116, 119, 121-26, 123, 125, 149, 149, 173, 193, 197, 198-208, 201, 203, 205, 207, 214, 215-16, 224-27, 224-33, 229, 230, 232, 233; plates 18-20, 32
    guidelines, 48, 200, 205, 208, 214, 215, 227
    overseas, 2, 15, 17, 17, 27, 35, 39, 90, 101, 101-03, 103, 110, 206
    see also epidemics
Disney, Walt, 128, 129
District of Columbia, 109, 120, 227
Dos Passos, John, xi, 35
Drew, Dr. Charles R., 134, 134
Dunant, Henry, 1, 10

East Germany, 190, 191
Eisenhower, Dwight D., 152, 203, 216
elderly, assistance to, ix, 127, 205, 215, 231, 240, 241
Elizabeth, Queen, 132
Elsey, George M., 186, 223, 224, 234, 243-44
epidemics, 20, 21, 25, 56, 59, 68, 82-83, 83, 84, 90, 178, 178, 179
Evansville Daily Journal, 16

Farrand, Dr. Livingston, 95, 97
Fay, Charles, 42
Fieser, James, 108, 122, 150, 151
Finland, 132
first aid, 119, 144, 149, 227, 230, 236; plate 35
    instruction, 21, 28, 33, 34, 39, 39-42, 41, 106, 114, 117, 118, 142, 196, 236, 237, 238, 241
    see also disaster relief; safety
Fisher, Harrison, plate 13
Flagg, James Montgomery, plate 23
Fontrese, Marguerite, 69
Foringer, A. E., 69; plate 11
Forrest City (Ark.), 122, 124
Fort Chaffee (Ark.), 222
Fort McKenzie (Ga.), 24
Fort McPherson (Ga.), 24
France, 5
    World War I and postwar, 72-76, 77, 78-80, 80, 85, 86, 88, 89
    World War II, 136, 137, 158, 160, 162, 165
Franco-Prussian War, 10, 11, 12, 12
Franz Ferdinand, Archduke, 57

Gainesville (Ga.), 125
Galle, Fortune, 69
Galveston (Tex.), 1-2, 19, 20
Gardner, Mrs. Florence, 174
Gardner, Harry, 70
Garfield, James A., 13
Geneva Convention: (1864), 1, 4, 5, 11, 12, 13, 13, 14 (1929), 163, 209
Germany, 59, 130, 131, 163, 165
Glenn, John M., 67
Grant, Ulysses S., 8
Gray Lady Service, 107, 114, 115, 164
Grayson, Adm. Cary T., 62
"Greatest Mother" theme, 69, 94; plates 11, 27
Greece, 138
Gruenther, Gen. Alfred M., 174, 190, 191
Guam, 232, 233
Guttridge, Mrs. Janette, 146

Hale, Marshall, 52
Haller, Gen., 98
Hamilton, Capt. R. Hayes, 92
handicapped and disabled (assistance and programs), 93, 115, 176, 194, 194, 196, 215, 238, 239, 241
    veterans, 56, 93, 93, 94, 167, 194; plate 15
    see also hospital recreation and rehabilitation programs
Harding, Warren, 52
Harper's Weekly, 9
Harriman, Mrs. E. H., 52
Harriman, E. Roland, 174, 177, 216, 243
Harrisburg (Pa.), 231
Hartford Post, 30
Hartford Times, 202
Hemingway, Ernest M., xi, 75
Hickman (Ky.), 48
Hildebrand, Mrs. Ruth, 174
Hillyer, Robert, 75
Hine, Lewis, 118
Hiroshima, 28, 29
Hitachi, Princess, 240
Holland, Dr. Jerome, 216, 224
Holmes, Dr. J. A., 42
Hope, Bob, 129
Hopkins, Harry, 122
hospital recreation and rehabilitation programs, 78, 78, 92, 93, 107, 114, 115, 163, 164, 164, 174, 174-76, 220, 221, 240, 241; see also handicapped and disabled
House, A. Sherbourne, 130
housing and shelter, 22, 31, 33, 38, 48, 104, 117, 119, 122, 124, 125, 190, 198, 201, 203, 204, 205, 222, 230, 231
Houston (Tex.), 20
Howe, Edward, 28
Hubbell, Dr. Julian B., 15, 17
Hughes, Col. J. L., 217
Hungarian revolution, 187, 187-89

Hurley, Edward N., 60

Indochinese refugees, 216, 222, 222, 223, 223
influenza epidemic (1918-19), 56, 68, 82-83, 83, 84
International Committee of the Red Cross, 143, 163, 165, 166, 188, 223
International Conference of the Red Cross: (1902), 27; (1934), 110; (1969), 209
International Red Cross, 1, 10, 12, 190, 220; see also Geneva Convention; League of Red Cross Societies
Italy, 73, 74, 75, 80, 157-59, 161, 161

Jacksonville (Fla.), 50, 100
Japan, 28, 29, 29, 101, 101, 102, 110, 145
    World War II, 144, 145, 146, 163, 174
Jersey City (N.J.), 171
Johnstown (Pa.), 1, 2, 22, 22, 31, 214, 225
Junior Red Cross, see youth

Kauffman, R. C., plate 28
Kay, Margery, plate 4
Kazakoff, Adm. N., 27
Keller, Helen, 194
Kennedy, Edward, 223
Kennedy, Robert, 191
Kerr, Donald, 163
Key West (Fla.), 199
Kimball, Red, 109
Knox, Mrs. Joan, 240
Korean War (and Korea), 168, 175, 179-82, 180-86, 185, 186

Lapham, E. G., 13
Law, Joseph, 100
League of Nations, 56, 87
League of Red Cross Societies, 56, 87, 88, 187, 206
Lejeune, Maj. John, 52
Leslies Weekly, 15
Lexington (Tenn.), 202
lifesaving, see safety
Lincoln, Abraham, 5, 6, 9
Logan, Mrs. John, 31
London, 132, 133, 152, 152
Long Beach (Calif.), 146
Longfellow, Comm. Wilbert E., 33, 50, 51, 98, 99
Lonoke (Ark.), 113
Los Angeles, 119, 149, 156
Louisville (Ky.), 123
Louisville Courier-Journal, 112
Lynch, Maj. Charles, 33

MacArthur, Gen. Douglas, 145, 179
McCarthy, Charlie, 129
McCracken, Dr. Henry Noble, 64
McGovern, George, 209

McKinley, William, 2, 23
McWilliams, Elizabeth, 84
Magee, Charles L., 34
Mahoney, William, plate 9
Maine, 23
Manila, 140, 167
Margo, Antoinette, 11
Marshall, Gen. George C., 143, 177, 179, 180
Matsukata, Count, 29
Mexico, 33, 53, 53, 54, 196
Michigan, 1, 14, 15, 15
military (assistance and programs), ix, 24, 42-43, 48, 95, 173, 190, 191, 233, 242
    canteens and clubmobiles, 55, 66, 69, 72, 72, 73, 87, 142, 155, 158, 158-60, 159, 161, 164, 184, 185
    home services (emergency and welfare), 72, 79, 80, 142, 148, 152, 154, 154, 155, 161, 162, 180, 181, 181, 217, 218, 218, 220, 221, 233
    recreation: service clubs and units, 152, 152, 153, 155, 159, 161, 179, 184, 185, 185, 211, 211, 219, 220, 221; Special Services Clubs, 179, 184; USO, 152, 184; see also canteens and clubmobiles above; hospital recreation and rehabilitation programs
    veterans, 95, 107, 115, 215, 217, 221; disabled, 56, 93, 93, 94, 167, 194; plate 15
    war relief, 10, 53, 55, 58, 220, 233; see also individual conflicts
Mills, Mrs. Kay, 174
Misquamicut (R.I.), 198
Mississippi River floods, 1, 16, 17, 48, 95, 104, 105, 121-24
Monaco, 138
Moton, Dr. Robert R., 104
motor services, 73, 119, 135
    Motor Corps, 55, 65, 84, 164, 166, 241
    see also ambulance services; blood programs and research; canteens, clubmobiles, and feeding vans
Muhall, Francis, 34
Murphy, Grayson M. P., 60

Newark (N.J.), 106, 194
New Orleans, 21, 198, 199
New Orleans Times-Picayune, 198
New York City, 39, 70, 71, 135, 147, 164, 193, 208, 228
    blood programs, 133, 134
    Institute for Crippled and Disabled Men, 94
New York Times, 51
New York World, 20, 27
Nicholson, James, 186
North American, 44
Norton, Charles D., 60, 61
nursing and medical assistance, 39, 45

nursing (cont'd)
  black nurses, 21, 68
  Civil War, 4, 5, 6, 6, 8, 9, 12,
    51
  disasters and epidemics, 17, 18,
    20, 21, 22, 25, 36, 49, 55,
    59, 82–83, 84, 90, 91, 102,
    105, 198, 201, 202, 206, 208
  by elephants, 27
  Franco-Prussian War, 10, 11,
    12
  Hungarian revolution, 188,
    189
  Indochinese refugees, 216,
    223, 223
  Korean War, 179, 180, 180,
    182, 182–84
  Mexican civil war, 33
  Russo-Japanese War, 28
  Spanish-American War, 2, 23,
    23–26
  Vietnam War, 209, 211, 213
  volunteer aides, 164, 168, 178,
    195, 196, 197, 241
  World War I and postwar, 55,
    58–60, 60, 63, 63, 65, 68,
    72, 74, 74–79, 78, 81, 81,
    83, 83, 84, 88–94, 98; plate
    4; idealized in song and
    story, 47; plates 3, 9
  World War II, 132, 133–36,
    134, 140, 142, 144–46,
    144–48, 155, 155–58, 158,
    161, 161–64, 164, 165, 168,
    168; plate 25
  see also blood programs and re-
    search; first aid; public health

O'Connor, Basil, 174, 176, 176,
  177
Ohio River floods, 16, 17, 48, 49,
  122–24

Paris, 85
Patterson, F. D., 153
Payne, John Barton, 95, 108–13,
  110, 127
Pearl Harbor, 144, 144
Pegler, Westbrook, 153
Pennsylvania Hillside Coal Com-
  pany, 39
Pershing, Gen. John, 54, 71
Pétain, Field Marshal Henri, 86
Peters, G. W., 19
Philadelphia, 22, 29
Philippines, 140, 140, 145, 146,
  167, 175, 175
Pickens, Dean, 151
Poincaré, Raymond, 86
Poland, 87, 90, 130, 130, 131,
  163, 169
posters, 42, 45, 63, 69, 70, 212,
  233; plates 8, 10, 12–30, 32–35
prisoners and juvenile offenders,
  215, 241, 242
  see also Bay of Pigs
prisoners of war: Korean War,
  185, 186, 186
  Vietnam War, 209, 217
  World War I, 80, 80

World War II, 142–43, 163,
  163, 165, 165, 166
Production Corps, 55, 65, 83, 133,
  142, 146, 147, 148, 164,
  168
Providence (R.I.), 126
public health (incl. Rural Nursing; Town and Country
  Nursing), 33, 40, 41, 44, 45,
  46, 46, 89, 95, 126, 127, 128,
  209, 210
  Cardio-Pulmonary Resuscita-
    tion, 237
  food and nutrition, 169, 171,
    215
  home nursing, 142, 146, 175,
    196, 241
  tuberculosis and Christmas
    Seals, 33, 39, 42–44
  see also blood programs and re-
    search; handicapped and dis-
    abled; nursing and medical
    assistance
Pullman Company, 40, 41
Putnam (Conn.), 202
Pyle, Ernie, 161

railroads, 39–41, 149
Ray, Lillie, 43
Red Cross Courier, 100, 179
Red Cross Magazine, 38; plates 5–7,
  11
Ridgway, Gen. Matthew B., 181
Riggs, Dr. Joseph K., 12
Robinson, Dr. G. Canby, 134
Rochester (N.Y.), 14, 15, 177
Rockefeller, John D., Jr., 61
Rockefeller Foundation, 52, 59
Rockwell, Norman, plates 5–7, 35
Rogers, Will, 108
Roosevelt, Franklin D., 58, 95–
  96, 108, 114, 119, 129, 137,
  141, 172
Roosevelt, Mrs. Franklin D., xi,
  120, 153
Roosevelt, Theodore, 3, 27, 30,
  31, 32, 35, 36
Russia, 2, 15, 17, 17, 27, 56, 59,
  90, 90–92
Russo-Japanese War, 28, 29

safety/safety instruction, 3, 33,
  38–41, 40, 42, 106, 215
  American First Aid Associa-
    tion, 3
  lifesaving and water safety, ix,
    33, 39, 50, 51, 98–100, 192,
    193, 196, 215, 236–39, 237,
    238, 241
  see also first aid
Sage, Mrs. Russell, 52
Sage Foundation, Russell, 67
St. Louis (Mo.), 84, 229
Saltsburg (Pa.), 122
Salvation Army, 20
San Francisco, 32, 33, 35, 35–38,
  36, 52, 65, 228
Schafer, A. L., 112
Scrymser, James A., 52
Seabrook, William, 75

Sea Islands (S.C.), 1–2, 18
Serbia, 59, 90
Service, Robert W.: Rhymes of a
  Red Cross Man, 56, 77, 161
Shields, Dr. Matthew J., 39, 40
Shreveport Times, 30
Smith, Jesse Wilcox, plate 14
Smith, Phyllis, 108
Soviet Union, 132, 163
Spanish-American War, 2, 23,
  23–27
Spieler, Daisy, 148
Stanton, Frank, 216, 234
Stimson, Henry, 159
Swift, Ernest J., 57
swimming instruction, see safety
Syracuse (N.Y.), 14, 15

Taft, William Howard, 44, 51,
  53, 60, 67, 97
Tamura, Gen. H., 163
Temple, Shirley, 121
Thomas, Jesse O., 150, 151
Thomas, Norman, 111
Thompson, J. D., 236
Three Mile Island (Pa.), 215–16,
  225
Tillinghast, B. F., 27
Titanic, 39
Tokyo, 101, 102, 110
Truman, Harry S., 143, 169, 176,
  176, 182, 216
tuberculosis, fight against, 33, 39,
  42–44

unemployment aid, 96, 108, 111,
  111–14, 116, 117, 117
United Daughters of the Confederacy, 52
United Nations, 223; see also Korean War
United States government (and
  the Red Cross), 2, 3, 23, 32
  Barton's efforts rebuffed, 1, 11,
    12
  charter, 217, 220, 233; (1900),
    2, 4, 29; (1905), 32, 33, 34,
    53; (1947), 173, 176, 176,
    243
  disaster relief, 32, 35, 36, 47,
    48, 48, 207, 208, 215, 230,
    231, 233
  financial accountability, 32, 35,
    234, 234
  financial aid from U.S. govern-
    ment refused, 95, 111, 112,
    113, 233
  first aid training for govern-
    ment workers, 115, 117
  Geneva Convention (1864), 1,
    4, 5, 11, 12, 13, 13, 14
  Indochinese refugees, 216,
    222, 222, 223, 223
  unemployment aid, 98, 108,
    111, 111–14, 116, 117, 117
  see also blood programs and re-
    search; military; under indi-
    vidual conflicts
United States Sanitary Commission, 5, 5, 6, 12

United Way (and community
  funds), 120, 173, 215, 233,
  233
USO, 152, 184

Van Reypen, Adm., 34
Varga, Msgr. Bela, 188
Vasilakos, Stefan, 120
Vera Cruz (Mex.), 53
Vietnam War, 184, 209, 209–13,
  217, 217–21, 220, 221; see
  also Indochinese refugees

Wadsworth, Eliot, 55, 60, 67, 97
war relief, 10, 53, 233
  concept of neutrality, 55, 58,
    220
  see also under individual con-
    flicts
Washington (D.C.), 21
  Red Cross headquarters, 32,
    34, 51, 51, 52
Washington Post, 109
water safety, see safety
Weatherford (Tex.), 64
Wedel, Mrs. Cynthia, 240
Weissmuller, Johnny, 100
Wesselius, Walter, 144
Wheeling (W. Va.), 105
Wichita Falls (Tex.), 224
Wilbur, Lawrence, plate 27
Wilkes-Barre, 231
Williams, Annie Laurie, 91
Wilmington (Del.), 197
Wilson, Mrs. Janet, 174
Wilson, Woodrow, 55, 60, 61,
  62, 64, 77, 109
Woman's Relief Corps, 52
Women's Central Association of
  Relief, 4
Worcester (Mass.), 201
World War I (and postwar), 33,
  55–56, 57, 57–83, 60–63,
  67, 68, 70–72, 74, 78, 84,
  85, 85–89, 86, 90, 91–94,
  95, 108; plates 3–6, 8–10, 12
World War II (and postwar), 96,
  101, 110, 129–32, 130–41,
  134, 137, 139–52, 144–49,
  152–72, 154, 157–59, 161,
  163–65, 168, 169, 183, 194;
  plates 22–31
Wyeth, N. C., plate 21

Yazoo (Miss.), 121
YMCA/YWCA, 41, 50, 92, 98,
  187, 238
youth, 17
  Boy Scouts, 50, 99
  Junior Red Cross, 55, 64, 83,
    106, 147, 148, 151, 167, 170,
    171, 195, 195, 202; plates 6,
    16, 17, 34
  New Pride, 241
  Student Reserve, plate 29
  Youth Services, 195, 196, 197,
    210, 219, 233, 241
  see also first aid; safety
Yugoslavia, 206

246